The Ultimate

Persian Cookbook

A Complete Guide to 111 Healthy and Delicious Persian Dishes

by

Slavka Bodic

Why this cookbook?

I was born in the Balkans. Specifically, I used to live in the former Yugoslavia and I currently reside in Serbia. While I was living in Yugoslavia, communist leader Tito promoted best possible relations with both East and West. As a part of his policy, he established a Non-Aligned Movement and an open country for students from many countries from Africa, Asia, and Middle East. This was the occasion when I was in contact with people from Iran for the first time and when I initially tasted delicious Persian dishes. When my children were later visiting Iran, they helped me to acquire a deeper understanding of the cuisine. Thus, you can bring an exotic and unique experience to your tables!

Again, my son and daughter brought me many recipes and some ingredients. I become quite interested to further experiment with help of my Persian friend who was living in my country for a long time. The key challenge was to develop all recipes, so they could be prepared in any kitchen. This cookbook is result of my year-long efforts and I deeply appreciate your honest feedback on Amazon.

After quite unexpected success of seven previous cookbooks from the Balkans, Caucasus, and Mediterranean regions, I decided to continue to share even more. I believe that exchanging cultural facets with others is the most beautiful experience in the world. For me, the food I love and the recipes I like and develop are vital to share. I hope you like this and other cookbooks that I'll publish in the coming months.

At the moment, you can check my Balkan Cookbook, Greek Cookbook, Serbian Cookbook, as well as 111 recipes for your Mediterranean diet. All cookbooks are available at the Amazon.

Once again, I'd be very grateful if you take the time to post a short review on Amazon.

Warmly,
Slavka Bodić

Table of Contents

Persian or Iranian?

People often believe that Persian and Iranian are the same term. Both terms are typically used to describe people from Iran, but it isn't entirely correct. Some clarification is needed in relation to this.

Persia was the Western official name for Iran until 1935, when term "Iran" came into existence. "Persia" refers to the well-known Persian Empire. Modern Iran was formed over the center of ancient Persia and exemplified the monarchy until end of the 1970s. In 1979, after the revolution, Iran became The Islamic Republic of Iran.

Iran has about 83 million inhabitants at the moment and 61% are ethnic Persians (16% Azerbaijani, 10% Kurd, 6% Lur, 2% Turkmen, 2% Baloch, 2% Arab). However, 53% speaks Persian language. Consequently, Iran and Persia are both equally used in a cultural context, while Iran is the only term for political perspective.

Persians aren't Arabs; only 2% or Arabs live in Iran. Arabs live in 22 countries of Middle East and North Africa, including countries that are neighbors of Iran (Iraq, Saudi Arabia and Kuwait).

If you're interested in this part of the world, I strongly recommend reading more about the Persian Empire and historical sites such as Persepolis.

Why Persian Food?

Persian cuisine is a result of a long interaction between local culinary culture and neighboring cuisines such as Turkish, Greek, Caucasian, Indian, and many more. As you'll discover in this cookbook, typical Persian dishes include rice, meat, vegetables, herbs and nuts. While saffron is typical Persian herb, there's no standard Persian fruit or vegetable, since many of them are widely used.

Persian dishes are quite easy to make; and, in most cases, a long list of ingredients means a lot of different spices. If some of them aren't available, they can be excluded. In other cases, amount of spices could be further adjusted, based on your tastes and preferences.

There are much more than only 111 recipes, but this is the best possible selection for traditional dishes, number and availability of ingredients, time needed for preparation, and simplicity. Please note that some traditional Persian ingredients are unavailable in the West and are subject to change for the most similar ingredients available.

Persian cuisine is one of those that you'll love for sure, regardless your age, sex, ethnicity or regular eating habits.

Noosh-e jan! (Bon appetit!)

Just in case ...

Cooking Measurement Chart

Weight

imperial	metric
1/2 oz	15 g
1 oz	29 g
2 oz	57 g
3 oz	85 g
4 oz	113 g
5 oz	141 g
6 oz	170 g
8 oz	227 g
10 oz	283 g
12 oz	340 g
13 oz	369 g
14 oz	397 g
15 oz	425 g
1 lb	453 g

Measurement

cup	onces	milliliters	tbsp.
8 cup	64 oz	1895 ml	128
6 cup	48 oz	1420 ml	96
5 cup	40 oz	1180 ml	80
4 cup	32 oz	960 ml	64
2 cup	16 oz	480 ml	32
1 cup	8 oz	240 ml	16
3/4 cup	6 oz	177 ml	12
2/3 cup	5 oz	158 ml	11
1/2 cup	4 oz	118 ml	8
3/8 cup	3 oz	90 ml	6
1/3 cup	2.5 oz	79 ml	5.5
1/4 cup	2 oz	59 ml	4
1/8 cup	1 oz	30 ml	3
1/16 cup	1/2 oz	15 ml	1

Temperature

fahrenheit	celsius
100 °F	37 °C
150 °F	65 °C
200 °F	93 °C
250 °F	121 °C
300 °F	150 °C
325 °F	160 °C
350 °F	180 °C
375 °F	190 °C
400 °F	200 °C
425 °F	220 °C
450 °F	230 °C
500 °F	260 °C
525 °F	274 °C
550 °F	288 °C

MAIN DISHES

Chicken apricots stir fry

Have you ever tried apricots and chicken in the same dish? If not, I guarantee that you'll adore this dish. As you may know, apricot was renowned in history as the "Armenian plum." If you like this fruit, check more in my Armenian cookbook!

Preparation time: 5 minutes
Cook time: 20 minutes
Nutrition facts: Calories 225/ carbs 14 g/Fat 6 g /Protein 27 g

Ingredients (4 servings)
1 pound chicken breast, cut into 2 inch cubes
4 large portabella mushrooms, cut into 2-inch cubes
4 oz dried apricots, coarsely chopped
1 cup cashews
¾ cup raisins
½ cup chicken broth
1 tablespoon brown sugar
2 teaspoons sweet paprika
½ teaspoon ground ginger
Oil
Salt and pepper

Preparation
Place a large pan over medium heat and heat a splash of oil in it. Add the chicken and brown it for 5-7 minutes and then add the mushrooms. Stir and cook them for 3 minutes. Stir in the apricots, brown sugar, raisins, paprika, ginger, and salt and pepper. Cook for 4-6 minutes. Stir in the broth and cook them for 7 minutes over high heat. Fold in the cashews.

Persian Fried Buns Stuffed with Ground Beef

I know that this dish may sound like an appetizer for some of you, but 450 cal per serving is quite enough to rank it in the main dish category. However, I'm preparing this often for parties and similar gatherings, since it takes less than an hour for preparation.

Preparation time: 15 minutes
Cook time: 40 minutes
Nutrition facts: Calories 453/ carbs 25 g/Fat 12g /Protein 30g

Ingredients (2 servings)
2 eggs
1 cup yogurt
1 package yeast
3 cups flour
3 tablespoons oil
½ teaspoon salt
1 tablespoon sugar
1 cup warm water

Filling
1 small onion
½ pound of ground beef
Pepper and salt to taste
2 cloves garlic
1 tablespoon tomato paste
¼ teaspoon turmeric
1 cup parsley
Olive oil
Yogurt (for dipping)

Preparation

In a medium-sized bowl, combine sugar, yeast, and water; allow it to stand for 5-6 minutes. In the same bowl, add eggs, flour, salt, yogurt, and oil and combine all ingredients. Knead the batter and allow it to rest for an hour.

In a pan, sauté the onions and garlic then add turmeric. Cook for 1 minute. Add the ground beef and parsley. Next, season with pepper and salt; once cooked, set aside.

With your fingers, roll the dough to make big balls; fill each ball with the stuffing. Fry the balls in oil until they turn golden brown. Serve on a plate with a bowl of yogurt for dipping.

Brick Red Whole Baked Chicken

Try this excellent chicken recipe that you can prepare in one hour. Don't forget to prepare the rice while baking the chicken!

Preparation time: 20 minutes
Cook time: 40-45 minutes
Nutrition facts: Calories 472/ carbs 32 g/Fat 10.2g /Protein 20g

Ingredients (6 servings)
1 whole chicken
2 tablespoons lemon juice
¼ teaspoon turmeric powder
¼ teaspoon ground cumin
¼ teaspoon cinnamon powder
¼ teaspoon red chili powder
1 teaspoon red food coloring
1 teaspoon salt
4 tablespoons olive oil

Preparation
Preheat the oven to 400 F. Wash and clean the chicken. Mix all the ingredients in a bowl except the chicken. Create small slits in the chicken skin. Rub the chicken well with the marinade and let it rest for 15-18 minutes. Place on a lined baking dish and bake for 40-45 minutes or until cooked through and golden on top. Remove from the oven and let it rest before serving with the jeweled Persian rice (see the separate recipe in this cookbook).

Lime and Herby Baked Fish

I've tried this recipe with many different fishes, and it's very hard to decide which one is the best. In turn, you can decide. It's quite important to leave on the room temperature a bit before serving.

Preparation time: 10 minutes
Cook time: 25 minutes
Nutrition facts: Calories 419/ carbs 18 g/Fat 11.2g /Protein 18g

Ingredients (2 servings)

2 whole fish
1 teaspoon parsley, chopped
1 teaspoon thyme, chopped
1 teaspoon rosemary sprigs
1 lime, cut into thin slices
2 tablespoon lime juice
2 tablespoon honey
1 teaspoon chili flakes
6-8 peppercorns
2 tablespoon olive oil
Black pepper to taste
Salt to taste

Preparation

Clean the fish and cut a few slits on the skin. Next, add to a baking tray. Add lime slices onto the slit areas of the fish and around the fish, too. Add the peppercorns and herbs around the fish. Add olive oil, salt, pepper, chili flakes, honey, and lime juice on top. Bake for 20 minutes. Lastly, let it rest for 10 minutes before serving.

Persian Lamb and Vegetables

Don't be discouraged with the amount of ingredients in this recipe. The majority are actually spices. I tried this recipe with other meat as well, but lamb is simply the best.

Preparation time: 15 minutes
Cook time: 70 minutes
Nutrition facts: Calories 511/ carbs 20 g/Fat 9.2g /Protein 21g

Ingredients (4 servings)
2 pounds lamb, cut into bite size chunks
1 cup potatoes, cut into wedges
1 cup pumpkin, cut into wedges
1 cup spinach
1 cup zucchini, cut into chunks
6 peppercorns
2 cinnamon sticks
4 bay leaves
1 tablespoon ginger paste
1 tablespoon garlic paste
2 large onions, sliced
1 teaspoon turmeric
1 teaspoon cumin
1 teaspoon red chili powder
2 tablespoon oil
4 cups water
Fresh rosemary sprig
Salt to taste

Preparation

In a large pot, add the oil. Fry the lamb and the onions until they get a brown color. Add the cumin, ginger paste, garlic paste, turmeric, red chili powder, and salt. Mix and add the cinnamon, bay leaves, and peppercorn. Next, toss well. Add ½ cup water and cook on high heat for 20 minutes. Then add the potatoes and pumpkin; cook for 15 minutes. Add the zucchini, and the water. Bring it to boil. Simmer for 10 minutes. Add the rosemary and spinach. Cook for another 11 minutes and serve hot.

Shredded Chicken with Barberry and Rice

Preparation time: 15 minutes

Cook time: 65 minutes

Nutrition facts: Calories 502/ carbs 26 g/Fat 19g /Protein 28g

Ingredients (2 servings)

1 onion (chopped)

½ teaspoon saffron

2 oz butter

2 skinless chicken fillets

¼ cups dried barberry (soak in water)

1 teaspoon salt

1 tablespoon lemon juice

2 tablespoon sugar

1 teaspoon turmeric

½ teaspoon turmeric

½ teaspoon black pepper

Preparation

Put the chopped onions in a pot and add salt, turmeric, pepper, and chicken. Pour water, enough to drown the chicken. Cook over medium heat until chicken is soft. Take the chicken out and shred it. Now, put it in a large pan and turn the heat in low. Add butter and mix until the butter dissolves. Set aside.

Pour the ground saffron into a cup and top up with hot water, up to one-quarter of the cup. Remove the barberries from the water and rinse. Put them in the pan, then add saffron water, and mix for a minute. Pour lemon juice and add sugar to the mixture. Stir until the sugar dissolves and the content blends thoroughly. Serve warm.

Chicken and Chickpea Rice

Chickpea seeds are high in protein and very healthy. They were domesticated in Turkey in Greece during the Neolithic period and are now very popular in this part of the world.

Preparation time: 120 minutes

Cook time: 15 minutes

Nutrition facts: Calories 423/ carbs 18 g/Fat 10.2g /Protein 38g

Ingredients (4 servings)

1 cup boiled chickpeas

1 pound chicken, cut into medium chunks

Fresh coriander, chopped

½ cup red onions, cut into wedges

4 green chilies

2 tablespoon butter

2 tablespoon oil

¼ teaspoon saffron mix with 1 tablespoon warm milk

1 cup yogurt

1 teaspoon ginger paste

1 teaspoon garlic paste

1 teaspoon red chili powder

1 tablespoon lemon juice

2 cups basmati rice

1 cup water

1 cup pomegranate seeds to serve

Salt and pepper to taste

Preparation

Marinate the chicken with salt, pepper, ginger paste, garlic paste, red chili powder, and yogurt. Soak rice in water for 12o minutes. Drain well and rinse off the water. In a deep dish, add the oil and the chicken with its marinated juice. Add the rice. Add the saffron mix, red onion, herbs, lemon juice, green chilies, butter, chickpeas, and water. Cover with a lid. Cook on medium heat for 30 minutes. Take off the heat and add the pomegranate seeds on top before serving.

Persian Shish Kabob

Kabob, kebab, chevap, cevap... There are many different terms for a similar type of dish. This is the Persian version and I must say it's quite delicious.

Preparation time: 10 minutes
Cook time: 30 minutes
Nutrition facts: Calories 297/ carbs 3 g/Fat 14 g /Protein 38 g

Ingredients (4 servings)
1 tablespoon salt
2 pounds beef tenderloin
1 onion, chopped
1/8 cup fresh lime juice
Ground black pepper

Preparation
Chop and cut the beef into one and a 1/2-inch cubes. Put in a bowl and add the salt, black pepper, lime juice, and onion. Mix thoroughly and refrigerate for several hours or overnight. Preheat the grill to high heat and weave the beef on skewers. Place about 6 to 8 on each skewer. Brush with oil and cook it on the grill 15 minutes or until fully done.

Persian Pan-Fried Chicken

Here's a quick simple, but delicious meal. If it's not possible to find Persian advieh, you can use Indian garam masala. Instead of feta, you can also serve with some other white cheese.

Preparation time: 8 minutes
Cook time: 25 minutes
Nutrition facts: Calories 509/ carbs 32 g/Fat 14 g /Protein 37g

Ingredients (2 servings)

2 chicken breasts
1 tablespoon Persian *advieh* seasoning (store-bought)
1½ tablespoon Persian dried lime, ground
½ teaspoon black pepper, freshly ground
1 teaspoon salt
1 tablespoon oil

Preparations

In a grinder, grind the Persian dried lime until it turns to a powder. In a small bowl, mix the Persian *advieh* seasoning, pepper, and salt. Cut each chicken in half and rub the *advieh* seasoning mixture. In a skillet, pour oil and sauté the chicken until golden brown. Remove from the skillet and drain the chicken on paper towels. Serve the chicken with tomato and feta salad on the side.

Duck Isfahan

Preparation time: 6 minutes

Cook time: 220 minutes

Nutrition facts: Calories 505/ carbs 28 g/Fat 20g /Protein 32g

Ingredients (8 servings)

8 duck legs

3 tablespoon canola oil

¼ cup of water, or as needed

3 tablespoon of olive oil, or more to taste

2 cups diced yellow onion

1 teaspoon ground turmeric

½ teaspoon ground cinnamon

6 cups chicken broth

¾ cup pomegranate molasses

¼ cup honey

3 cups chopped walnuts

¼ cup raisins

¼ cup chopped dried apricots

Salt and pepper to taste

Preparation

Salt and pepper the duck legs. Season all the duck legs all over with salt and black pepper. Heat the oil in a pot and brown the duck legs for 8-10 minutes, 4-5 minutes each side. Transfer the duck to a platter and save the fat in a bowl.

Bring ¼ cup of water to boil in the same pot and scrap the brown bits. Set aside. Combine 2 tablespoons of duck fat and 3 tablespoon of olive oil in a Dutch oven.

Sauté the onions for 10 minutes. Stir in the spices and cook for 1 minute. Add the broth, pomegranate molasses, honey, and the ¼ cup reserved water and heat to a simmer. Place the walnuts in a food processor and finely grind. Pour honey, all chicken broth, pomegranate molasses, and the reserved water mixture from the skillet into the onions, and then bring to a simmer.

Stir the ground walnuts in a skillet and then add them to the broth. Stir in the raisins and chopped dried apricots. Cover the pot and simmer for 3 hours. Place the duck legs on a platter. Bring the sauce to a boil and cook 9-12 minutes. Pour the sauce over the duck legs.

Persian Chicken and Mushrooms

I guess that you've likely tried many combinations of chicken and mushrooms, but this one is really interesting. I experimented with many different types of mushrooms, but champignons are always a good and available choice.

Preparation time: 15 minutes
Cook time: 55 minutes
Nutrition facts: Calories 410/ carbs 10 g/Fat 9g /Protein 20g

Ingredients (4 servings)
2 egg yolks
24 oz. mushrooms
8 chicken thighs
2 medium onions
1 tablespoon flour
4 garlic cloves
4 tablespoon lemon juice
2 tablespoons saffron
Vegetable oil (for frying)
Pepper and salt (to taste)

Preparation
Sauté the garlic and onion in a skillet until translucent; cook for 5 minutes. In the same skillet, add the water and chicken thighs that were seasoned with pepper and salt. Cook for 30 minutes and set aside. Sauté the mushrooms in the same skillet until the juices evaporate. Add flour, lemon juice and saffron; then season with pepper and salt, cook for 10 minutes. In a bowl, beat the eggs and pour into the skillet. Next, cook for 15 minutes and remove from the heat. Serve the stew in a large bowl and pair it with cooked rice.

Lamb Kebabs with Yogurt and Mint

My suggestion for this unique kebab is 2 tablespoons of chopped mint, but you can also increase the amount to the taste.

Preparation time: 10 minutes
Cook time: 30 minutes
Nutrition facts: Calories 498/ carbs 22 g/Fat 10.4g /Protein 32g

Ingredients (4 servings)

1 tablespoon mint sauce (store-bought)

13 oz. lean lamb

5 ½ oz. low-fat natural yogurt

14 oz. couscous (whole grain)

Freshly ground black pepper (to taste)

2 small onions

1 green pepper

2 tablespoon chopped mint

1 garlic clove

Lemon wedges

Salt (to taste)

Preparation

Preheat grill for the skewers. In a medium-sized bowl, combine the mint sauce, mint, garlic and lamb. Ensure that the lamb is fully covered with the mint sauce mixture and then refrigerate for 12 minutes. In a large bowl, add the couscous and pour boiling water; allow rice to absorb water before seasoning it with pepper and salt. Thread the onion wedges and lamb on metal skewers and grill for 10 minutes. Serve the kebabs with the cooked couscous and lemon wedges.

Persian Venison Pita

Preparation time: 125 minutes

Cook time: 10 minutes

Nutrition facts: Calories 412/ carbs 16 g/Fat 12g /Protein 28g

Ingredients (3 servings)

3 pounds venison

1 package pita bread

2 teaspoons ground dried rosemary

2 tablespoons olive oil

2 teaspoons dried marjoram

1 tablespoon minced garlic

1½ tablespoons ground cumin

1 tablespoon red wine vinegar

1 tablespoon dried oregano

Pepper and Salt (for seasoning)

Preparation

In a large ceramic bowl, add the rosemary, garlic, cumin, marjoram, red wine vinegar, venison strips, oregano, pepper, and salt. Toss to coat the meat. Cover the ceramic bowl and refrigerate the marinade for about 130 minutes. Cook the venison strips in a large skillet for about 9 minutes or until golden brown. Layer the meat on top of the warmed pita bread and serve.

Lamb Burger on Pita Bread

Preparation time: 15 minutes

Cook time: 30 minutes

Nutrition facts: Calories 511/ carbs 17 g/Fat 9g /Protein 18g

Ingredients (6 servings)

½ pound lean ground lamb

2 cloves garlic

1 slice pita bread

½ onion

½ pound lean ground beef

½ teaspoon ground allspice

½ teaspoon salt

1 dash ground cumin

½ teaspoon ground coriander

½ teaspoon ground black pepper

½ teaspoon dried Persian *advieh* seasoning

Preparation

Preheat a grill and grease the grate with oil. In a large bowl, combine ground lamb, garlic, onion, ground beef and breadcrumbs. Season it with salt, allspice, coriander, pepper and *advieh* seasoning. Knead the mixture and shape into 4 thin patties. Grill the patties for 8 minutes on each side. Transfer to a plate and serve.

Persian Kebabs with Sauce and Crumbled Feta

Preparation time: 10 minutes

Cook time: 30 minutes

Nutrition facts: Calories 521/ carbs 21 g/Fat 18g /Protein 25g

Ingredients (6 servings)

Marinade

¾ cup balsamic vinaigrette dressing

1 tablespoon dried oregano

3 tablespoons lemon juice

4 chicken breast halves

½ teaspoon black pepper, freshly ground

Sauce

1 tablespoon lemon juice

1 cup plain yogurt

1 teaspoon salt

¼ cup sour cream

½ cup shredded cucumber

1 teaspoon olive oil

1 tablespoon chopped fresh dill

1 clove garlic

Salt

½ tablespoon rice vinegar

Ground black pepper

1 cup feta cheese (crumbled)

½ teaspoon Persian *advieh* seasoning (store-bought)

1 heart of romaine lettuce

4 large pita bread rounds

1 red onion
½ cup Kalamata olives
½ cup pepperoncini
1 tomato

Preparation

Preheat your outdoor grill and set the temperature to high heat. Prepare the marinade by placing the oregano, juice from ½ lemon, and balsamic vinaigrette in a bowl. Transfer the marinade in a Ziploc bag then place the chicken inside. Refrigerate the marinating chicken for an hour then set aside.

Meanwhile, in a medium bowl, toss shredded cucumber and salt; allow it to rest for 5 minutes. After 5 minutes, squeeze excess water and add in the rice vinegar, olive oil and lemon juice. Season it with fresh dill, *advieh* seasoning, pepper, salt, and garlic; mix well and set aside.

Remove the chicken from the Ziploc bag and place on the grill grate. Grill the chicken for 9 minutes and rest for 11 minutes when done. Slice the chicken into thin strips and add them into the pita rounds. Grill for 2 minutes then remove from the grill. Arrange the cooked pita and layer with chicken strips, tomato, lettuce, pepperoncini, and Kalamata olives. Serve with the sauce and feta cheese in a separate bowl.

Chicken Gyro with Persian Yogurt

Similar to Greek *gyros*, this one offers something unique and adjusted in the local Persian cuisine. Apart from chicken, you can use other types of meat as well.

Preparation time: 20 minutes
Cook time: 20 minutes
Nutrition facts: Calories 534/ carbs 15 g/Fat 20g /Protein 38g

Ingredients (6 servings)

6 pita bread rounds

1 ¼ pounds chicken breast

1 ½ teaspoons dried dill weed

1 teaspoon white vinegar

1 container Persian yogurt

1 tablespoon and 1 teaspoon extra-virgin olive oil

1 teaspoon lemon juice

1 cucumber

1 tablespoon dried oregano

Pepper and salt

6 cloves garlic

1 tomato

Juice of 1 lemon

2 teaspoons red wine vinegar

1 red onion

Preparation

Preheat your broiler and adjust the rack by 6 inches away from the heat. In a blender, purée 2 cloves of garlic, cucumber, Persian yogurt, dill weed, white vinegar, a tablespoon olive oil, a tablespoon of lemon juice, pepper, and salt.

Blend the ingredients until smooth and set aside. In a ceramic bowl, whisk the juice of 1 lemon, pepper, 4 cloves of minced garlic, 2 tablespoon olive oil, oregano, red wine vinegar, salt and oregano. Once you have combined the next batch of ingredients, stir in the chicken; refrigerate the marinade. Remove the chicken from the marinade and transfer to a baking sheet. Broil the chicken for 4 minutes per side until it turns light brown. As soon as the chicken is done, allow it to rest for 6-7 minutes.

Meanwhile, heat a large skillet and add 1 teaspoon of olive oil; next, place the pita bread. Warm the pita for about 2 minutes and then top it with the chicken strips, tomato, lettuce, onions, and yogurt sauce.

Lamb Pita with Cucumber Yogurt

Preparation time: 10 minutes
Cook time: 20 minutes
Nutrition facts: Calories 602/ carbs 22 g/Fat 15g /Protein 31g

Ingredients (6 servings)
1 teaspoon onion powder
2 cloves garlic
1 pound lean ground lamb
1½ teaspoons dried oregano
¾ teaspoon pepper
1 teaspoon salt
Cucumber yogurt sauce (store-bought)
Tomato slices (for topping)
Pita bread

Preparation
Preheat your broiler to a medium to high heat. In a small bowl, combine the ground lamb, salt, pepper, crushed garlic, onion powder and crushed oregano. Shape the well-combined lamb mixture into patties and broil for 11 minutes. Once the patties are cooked, serve on pita bread and top with onions, sliced tomatoes and drizzle cucumber yogurt sauce on top.

Jeweled Persian Rice Served with Whole Chicken (*Morasa Polo*)

If you want a real taste of Persia, this is dish for you. It takes some time to prepare and a bit more ingredients than usual, but you won't regret it.

Preparation time: 60 minutes
Cook time: 70 minutes
Nutrition facts: Calories 532/ carbs 33 g/Fat 9g /Protein 22g

Ingredients (6 servings)

3 cups long grain white rice
Plenty of water for washing and soaking
1 teaspoon salt, for soaking
8 cups water, for cooking
2 teaspoons salt, for cooking
2 tablespoons olive oil
¼ teaspoon ground cinnamon
½ cup barberries, blanched and drained
¼ teaspoon turmeric powder
½ pound carrots, peeled and julienned into 3-inch long slices
½ cup blanched and slivered pistachios
½ cup blanched and slivered
½ cup chopped walnuts
½ cup raisins or sultanas
A few saffron strands
¼ teaspoon cumin
¼ teaspoon coriander powder
Salt and pepper to taste
5 tablespoons warm water
1 cup fresh pomegranate seeds
Kafgir (Persian rice serving spatula) or a slotted spoon
A wet tea towel

Preparation

Clean the rice and transfer to a large bowl to wash. You'll notice the water will have turned murky. Repeat until the water is clear. Add 1 teaspoon of salt to the soaking rice and leave uncovered for an hour. Bring 8 cups of water and 2 teaspoons of salt to a boil. Cook rice in the water until there is just a bite to it. The best way to check for the right amount of cooking is to take a grain between your fingers and mash it. If two or three rings like disc stand out and aren't mashed, the rice is done. Drain but don't run cold water over the rice.

Mix 5 tablespoons of water and the saffron. Set aside. In a pan, stir fry carrots in the olive oil until just tender. Lower the heat and add the cinnamon powder, pistachios, almonds, walnuts, coriander powder, red chili powder, cumin, salt, and pepper. Remove from heat. In a large pot, heat the oil and saffron water until boiling. Add half the rice and layer with carrot, walnuts, almonds, and pistachio mix. Add the second layer of rice and top with barberries and raisins. Lower the heat under the pot.

Wrap a tea towel under the lid and tie it up on top of the lid. Cover the pot to enclose steam inside it. This helps the rice fluff up as well. Cook for 40 minutes on low heat. During this time, don't stir the rice. When the time is up, open the lid and let it cool for a while. On kitchen counter, place the other wet tea towel. Move your rice pot and place it on the towel. You'll hear an instant sizzling sound. This is a good indication of the golden crust at the bottom. Let it rest on the towel for another 6 minutes. Once slightly cool, now mix the rice with *kafgir* to combine all the ingredients. Garnish with fresh pomegranate seeds and serve with the baked chicken.

Persian Chicken (*Morgh*)

Preparation time: 8 minutes
Cook time: 40 minutes
Nutrition facts: Calories 520/ carbs 20 g/Fat 22g /Protein 37g

Ingredients (4 servings)

¼ cups lemon juice
4 skinless chicken thighs
1 tablespoon turmeric
2 onions (1 chopped)
1 tablespoon tomato paste
4 tablespoon oil
½ teaspoon ground saffron
Water
Salt and black pepper

Preparation

Put the pieces of chicken parts in a pot and add the chopped onion. Include salt, pepper, and a half of the turmeric. Pour water into the pot that the chicken pieces are almost submerged underneath it. Cover the pot and cook over medium heat. Meanwhile, grate the other onion. Put it in a pan, pour some oil and add the black pepper and the other half turmeric. Wait until the color of the onion changes to golden. Then add tomato paste and stir. Leave the content and go back to the chicken pieces. Pour some oil into another frying pan and heat. Remove the chicken pieces when they are tender put them in the pan. Fry over medium heat until the color changes to light brown.

Don't get rid of the water the chicken is cooked in, since you'll need it later. Get the onion and tomato paste mixture and pour it on top of the chicken pieces. Make sure every piece is covered. Get a cup of water from the pot you cooked the chicken in and add it to the chicken. Put saffron and lemon juice. Cover and cook over low heat until the sauce gets thick. Garnish with parsley, lemon pieces, and French fries.

Persian Tomato Rice (*Estamboli Polow*)

Preparation time: 10 minutes
Cook time: 80 minutes
Nutrition facts: Calories 424/ carbs 21 g/Fat 10g /Protein 25g

Ingredients (4 servings)

3 potatoes (peeled and cubed)

2 cups long grain rice

1 pound ground beef

1 onion (diced)

1 teaspoon turmeric

2 tablespoon tomato paste

¼ teaspoon ground saffron (dissolve in 4 tablespoons hot water)

Salt

Black pepper

Vegetable oil

Water

Preparation

Pour 3 tablespoon oil in a pan and heat over medium heat. Add the diced onions and sauté until they become tender. Put the ground beef and mix until it turns light brown. Add black pepper, salt, and turmeric. Mix thoroughly. Add the peeled and cubed potatoes and cook for 5 minutes.

Add tomato paste and stir for 3 minutes. Reduce the heat and cook for an additional 5 minutes. Take the pot off the heat and keep. Grab another pot and pour 6 cups of water into it. Boil over medium heat. After that, pour rice into the water and leave until the outside layer of the rice is tender, but the middle is still hard. Drain the grains in a colander and rinse with water. Place the pot back on the cooker, turn the heat to medium and add 2 tablespoons of oil. Pour a layer of rice into it. Now, put a layer of meat and potato sauce. Add half of the saffron water too. Continue this process, but you should ensure that you end with a layer of rice. Pour the remaining half of saffron water on the top. Turn down the heat, cover, and leave to cook for 60 minutes.

Persian Herbed Frittatas with Fenugreek (*Kookoo Sabzi*)

This meal could be served for breakfast as well, but it's more common to have it as a part of dinner or lunch. As one of my favorite dishes, this one is great to experiment with other leaves, but fenugreek is the best one.

Preparation time: 10 minutes
Cook time: 45 minutes
Nutrition facts: Calories 523/ carbs 20 g/Fat 10g /Protein 31g

Ingredients (10 servings)

2 oz cilantro leaves, finely chopped

12 eggs, beaten

2 tablespoons olive oil (set more aside for greasing)

2 teaspoon flour

2 bunches scallions, chopped

1 teaspoon baking powder

2 tablespoons crumbled, dried fenugreek leaves

6 oz parsley, chopped

Ground black pepper

Salt

Preparation

Preheat oven to 375 F. Pour olive oil inside a skillet and heat over medium-high. Put parsley, scallions, and cilantro. Cook and stir constantly for about 6 minutes, just enough time until the content starts to droop. Take the skillet off the heat and leave the content to cool a little. While this is going on, grab a 12-cup muffin and grease with the oil. Break the eggs into a bowl and beat; add flour, baking powder, fenugreek leaves, salt, and pepper to season and taste. Go back to the herbs in the skillet and pour them into the egg mixture. Divide the mixture among the muffin cups. Leave to bake for 20-25 minutes until get the eggs to puff and color change to golden. Remove the muffin tin from the oven afterward and put on a rack. Let cool and then serve.

Herbed Rice with Fish Tahdig (*Sabzi Polo ba Tahdig-e Mahi*)

Preparation time: 15 minutes

Cook time: 150 minutes

Nutrition facts: Calories 513/ carbs 22 g/Fat 14g /Protein 21g

Ingredients (4 servings)

2 1-pound whole branzino (scaled, cleaned, butterflied, and fins removed)

2 cups dill, finely chopped

2 ½ cups extra-long white basmati rice

2 ¼ cups cilantro leaves, finely chopped

2 ¼ cups parsley leaves, finely chopped

¼ teaspoon saffron, ground gently with your fingers

½ cups finely chopped chives

Salt, to taste

Freshly ground black pepper

3 garlic cloves, thinly sliced

2 teaspoon fenugreek leaves, dried

1 tablespoon lemon zest, grated

¼ cup olive oil

2 teaspoons fresh lemon juice

¼ cup clarified unsalted butter

Preparation

Put rice in a bowl and pour water to cover it. Rinse with your hands and then remove the water. Do this until the water becomes clear. Add 2 fresh cups of water, put 2 tablespoons salt, and mix until it mixes with the water. Soak the rice for an hour. Pour 12 cups of water in a pot and bring to a boil over high heat. Put ¼ cup salt and mix with the water. Remove the water from the rice and pour into the pot. Stir lightly. Keep an eye on it and remove any foam that springs up. When the grain of rice starts to pop up, wait for four minutes. Taste the rice and see if it's soft on the outside and a little hard on the inside. Drain and rinse immediately with water. Get a small bowl and pour the ground saffron into it. Top up with ¼ cup of hot water. Use a bigger bowl and mix the cilantro, parsley, chives, dried dill, and fenugreek. Remove 2 cups of rice and keep. Pour the remaining rice into the mixture and mix with your hand. Taste and season with salt if you need to. Get the two fishes and season inside out with ¼ cup olive oil, black pepper, and salt. Fill the cavities with lemon zest, garlic and fresh dill. Finally, sprinkle with 1 teaspoon fresh lemon juice.

Put ¼ clarified butter, 3 tablespoons olive oil and 1 tablespoon saffron water in a big pot and put to medium-high heat. When the mixture starts to hiss, put the fishes and fry for 5-6 minutes. Place one fish at one side of the pot and the other at the other side. Then disperse the plain rice you had set aside on the fish. Next, calmly push the rice down the sides as you do so. Top the fishes and the rice with the herb rice. Gently dig some holes in the rice, but make sure not to reach the fish-*tahdig* layer. Put the pot cover on and cook on medium-high heat for about 10 minutes, which should be enough to set the *tahdig*.

Meanwhile, scoop 2 tablespoons of clarified butter into a small pot and melt. Next, add to the saffron water formerly set aside. Remove the cover from the pot the rice is cooking, making sure that you don't release the condensation back into the rice. Sprinkle the butter and saffron mixture on the rice. Cloak the cover with a kitchen towel, making sure it isn't loose to avoid a fire incident. Return the cover to the pot and reduce the heat to medium. Cook for 10 minutes, by then, steam should be coming out from the sides of the pot. Reduce the heat again and continue to cook. Turn the pot at intervals until the rice is soft; the fish is completely cooked and the *tahdig* is hard and crunchy. This should take about 37-42 minutes.

Fill the sink of with water and dump the bottom of the pot in it for a short time. Put a flat dish over the pot. You need to work fast here; turn the pot over to release the rice and *tahdig*. You should hear a sound when it releases. Remove the pot and serve.

Stuffed Grape Leaves (*Dolmah*)

These are highly popular meal in the Mediterranean region, but also in the Middle East and Caucasus regions. So far, I've tried more than 30 version of the same meal. The Persian one is really great.

Preparation time: 20 minutes
Cook time: 45 minutes
Nutrition facts: Calories 542/ carbs 21 g/Fat 21 g /Protein 34g

Ingredients

1 pound ground beef
2 cloves garlic, peeled and finely chopped
1⁄4 cup olive oil
Grape leaves, rinsed and stem removed
1⁄2 cup freshly squeezed lemon juice
1 cup diced yellow onion
1⁄2 scallions, chopped
1⁄3 cup split green peas
2⁄3 cup basmati rice, rinsed
1⁄2 cup fresh dill, finely chopped
1⁄2 cup fresh tarragon, finely chopped
1 teaspoon ground cinnamon
1⁄4 teaspoon saffron threads
1⁄4 cup sugar

Instructions

Heat the oil in a large saucepan. Add garlic, onions, and scallions and cook 5-6 minutes or until soft. Add the beef and cook until browned, another 5-6 minutes. Add dill, saffron, and tarragon. Add salt and pepper to taste. Add the rice and peas as well as 2 cups water. Cook covered until water is absorbed, about 40-50 minutes and then remove from heat. Stir in chopped parsley and cinnamon.

Take one flatten leaf and place about 2 tablespoons rice mixture in center and fold bottom of leaf over filling. Then fold in sides and roll into tight cylinder. Lay extra leaves over bottom of a Dutch oven, and then tightly layer rolls, seam-side down, on top. In a bowl, combine sugar and lemon juice and pour over the rolls. Cover tightly. Cook at medium-low heat for 48-52 minutes. Allow to cool before serving.

Persian Potato Pancakes (*KooKoo Sibzamini*)

Preparation time: 15 minutes

Cook time: 40 minutes

Nutrition facts: Calories 467/ carbs 20 g/Fat 12g /Protein 24g

Ingredients (6 servings)

4 large potatoes

1 tablespoon flour

¼ teaspoon turmeric

¼ ground saffron

Salt and pepper to taste

4 beaten eggs

½ cup canola oil

Preparation

Cut potatoes in half before placing them in a pot of salted water. Bring the water to a boil. Next, cook on low heat for 28-32 minutes, until the potatoes are done. Let them cool before peeling. Grate and place in a bowl. Add the flour, turmeric, saffron, salt and pepper in a bowl. Stir in the potatoes and eggs and stir well. Heat the oil in a skillet. Form 6 patties and fry them for 5 minutes, then flip the patties, and fry for another 5 minutes.

Eggplant Mirza

This one is super easy to make with just limited time. Many toppings could be added to this dish, but basil is my favorite one.

Preparation time: 15 minutes
Cook time: 30 minutes
Nutrition facts: Calories 476/ carbs 17 g/Fat 10g /Protein 20g

Ingredients (4 servings)

4 eggplants
2 tablespoons butter
1 diced onion
4 minced garlic cloves
6 diced tomatoes.
2 tablespoon lemon juice
7 eggs
3 tablespoons chopped basil
Salt and pepper to taste
Dash of cumin

Preparation

Preheat the broiler. Line a baking sheet with foil. Use a fork to pierce into the eggplants skin a few times. Place the eggplants on the baking sheet. Broil for 19-21 minutes. Let the eggplants cool. Peel and dice the eggplants. Melt the butter in a skillet over medium-low heat and sauté the onion and garlic for 5 minutes. Add the tomatoes, salt, pepper, cumin, and lemon juice and stir well. Add the eggplant to the mixture. Add the eggs and scramble for 5 minutes. Top with chopped basil.

Persian Spinach and Eggs (*Nargesi*)

Preparation time: 5 minutes

Cook time: 15 minutes

Nutrition facts: Calories 449/ carbs 27 g/Fat 12g /Protein 35 g

Ingredients (1 serving)

1 tablespoon olive oil

3 tablespoons diced onion

2 minced garlic cloves

2 cups chopped spinach

Salt and pepper to taste

½ teaspoon mint

1 egg

¼ cup plain Greek yogurt

1 sliced tomato

Dash of salt

Preparation

Heat the oil in a skillet. Sauté the onion for 5 minutes. Stir in the garlic and cook for another 3 minutes. Add the spinach and stir 5-6 minutes or until it wilts. Season with salt, pepper and mint. Transfer the spinach to a plate and keep warm. Add the egg to the skill and season as necessary. Scramble the egg but keep it soft. Stir the yogurt into the scrambled egg and cook for 3-4 minutes. Serve the egg on top of the spinach. Slice the tomato thin and sprinkle with salt. Transfer to the plate with the eggs and spinach.

Persian Chicken with Saffron

Preparation time: 10 minutes

Cook time: 30 minutes

Nutrition facts: Calories 564/ carbs 26 g/Fat 20g /Protein 40g

Ingredients (6 servings)

6 chicken thighs

2 diced onions

1 tablespoon curry

Salt and pepper to taste

1 tablespoon olive oil

¾ cup chopped dates

3 tablespoons lemon juice

½ teaspoon saffron

1 diced fresh tomato

Preparation

Add the chicken and 1 onion to a pot. Season with salt, pepper, and curry. Cover the chicken with water and cover the pot and simmer for 11-12 minutes. Heat the olive oil. Fry the remaining onion for 5 minutes. Set aside. Transfer the chicken in the same skillet and fry for 9-11 minutes. Keep the water. Add the chopped dates to the skillet. Use a cup of the reserved "chicken water" and stir in the saffron and lemon juice. Pour the liquid into the skillet. Add the diced tomato and cover your skillet and simmer for 12 minutes.

Chicken with Pomegranate
(*Khoresht Fesenjan*)

Preparation time: 7 minutes
Cook time: 160 minutes
Nutrition facts: Calories 611/ carbs 30 g/Fat 16g /Protein 39g

Ingredients (12 servings)

¼ cup canola oil
3 sliced onions
3 pounds cubed chicken
2 cups chicken broth
2½ cups pomegranate molasses
3 cups chopped walnuts
1 teaspoon cinnamon
1 teaspoon nutmeg
2 tablespoon lemon juice
2 tablespoon sugar
1-2 saffron threads
Salt and pepper to taste

Preparation

Heat the oil in a skillet. Sauté the onions on low heat for 20 minutes or until caramelized. Pour in the chicken broth and bring to a boil. Lower the heat and simmer for 30 minutes. Preheat the oven to 325 F. Place the walnuts and pomegranate paste in a food processor and blend until almost liquid. Add the walnut/pomegranate to the chicken mixture. Stir in the cinnamon, nutmeg, lemon juice, sugar, saffron, salt, and pepper and combine well. Transfer the chicken mixture to a baking dish. Cover the dish loosely with aluminum foil. Bake for 120 minutes and serve.

Persian Rice (*Chelo*)

Preparation time: 15 minutes

Cook time: 70 minutes

Nutrition facts: Calories 449/ carbs 27 g/Fat 11g /Protein 14g

Ingredients (8 servings)

1 pinch ground cumin

2 tablespoons butter

2 cups rinsed basmati

1 russet potato

¼ cup of sliced butter

½ teaspoon turmeric

1 ½ tablespoons hot water

1 tablespoon chopped parsley, or to taste

Salt to taste

Preparation

Cook the rice in your pot of salted water for 6 minutes. Drain and set aside. Pour the water and the salt to a boil in your pot and then add rice. Stir for 7 minutes. Slice the potato as thin as possible. Heat the butter in a pot. Arrange the potato in a single layer and season with salt and cumin. Cook on low for 6 minutes. Arrange the cooked rice over the potatoes. Place the butter slices over the rice. Season with turmeric. Cover the pot with a towel and steam the dish for 50 minutes. Transfer the Persian rice into a bowl.

Persian Herbed Rice

Preparation time: 15 minutes

Cook time: 30 minutes

Nutrition facts: Calories 465/ carbs 23 g/Fat 9g /Protein 14g

Ingredients (6 servings)

3 cups white basmati rice

3 minced garlic cloves

2 cup (or more) chopped dill, cilantro, mint, and chives

5 fenugreek leaves

1 cup butter

1 teaspoon grapeseed or olive oil

Salt as needed

Dash of saffron

Preparation

Rinse the rice. Place the rice in a bowl of salted water and soak for 55–60 minutes. Retain ¼ cup chopped herb for later. Place the mint, dill, cilantro, chives, and fenugreek leaves in a food processor and chop to a course. Cook the rice in a pot of salted water for 10 minutes and drain. Stir in the chopped herbs and garlic and combine well. Season with salt and add the saffron. Stir in the butter and cook on low for 19-22 minutes. Garnish with saffron and the herbs.

Green Bean Rice (*Lubia Polo*)

Preparation time: 15 minutes
Cook time: 70 minutes
Nutrition facts: Calories 495/ carbs 23 g/Fat 17g /Protein 29g

Ingredients (6 servings)

1 pound ground lamb

1 chopped onion

3 minced garlic cloves

1 tablespoon turmeric

4 cups chicken broth

1 cup tomato sauce

1 pound green beans cut into pieces

½ chopped green bell pepper

3 cups rinsed basmati rice

3 tablespoons vegetable oil

Preparation

Brown the lamb in a non-stick pot for 6 minutes and drain the grease. Add the onions and garlic and cook for another 6 minutes. Add the turmeric, broth, and tomato sauce. Stir in the green beans and chopped pepper. Simmer for 22 minutes or until beans are cooked. Stir the rice into the mixture and place a lid on the pot. Simmer for 16 minutes to let the liquid be absorbed, but don't overcook the rice.

Place the mixture in a bowl and heat the oil in the same pot. Transfer the bean/rice mixture back to the pot. Cover the pot with a towel and add the lid. Lastly, simmer for 29-32 minutes before serving.

Rice with Fava Beans (*Baqala Polo*)

Preparation time: 15 minutes

Cook time: 45 minutes

Nutrition facts: Calories 514/ carbs 21 g/Fat 10g /Protein 32g

Ingredients (6 servings)

2 cups white basmati rice

3 pounds fresh fava beans

½ cup olive oil

1 cinnamon stick

1 leek, finely chopped

4 cloves garlic, peeled and crushed

2 teaspoons salt

½ teaspoon freshly ground pepper

¼ teaspoon turmeric

2 tablespoons ground cardamom

2 tablespoons rose water

3 cups water

3 cups parsley, chopped

½ teaspoon ground saffron dissolved in 2 tablespoons rose water

Preparation

Wash and drain the rice. Remove the second skin of fava beans. Heat ¼ cup oil in a large pot over medium-high heat until very hot. Add the leek, cinnamon stick, and garlic. Stir and fry for 5 minutes or until the leek is wilted. Add the rice, salt, pepper, rose water, turmeric, cardamom, and stir and fry for another 1 minute. Add the water, tip in fava beans and bring back to a boil, stirring gently twice to loosen any grains that may have stuck to the bottom of the pot. Cover firmly with a lid and reduce heat to medium and cook for 15 minutes or less, until all the water has been absorbed. Add the dill and fluff.

Drizzle the remaining oil and the saffron-infused rose water over the rice. Reduce heat to low and cook covered for another 11-12minutes. Remove the pot from heat and allow to cool, still covered, for 8 minutes and then serve.

STEWS

Persian Herb Stew

Preparation time: 20 minutes

Cook time: 200 minutes

Nutrition facts: Calories 345/ carbs 34 g/Fat 16g /Protein 22 g

Ingredients (4 servings)

4 cups finely chopped fresh parsley

3 cups finely chopped fresh cilantro

2 cups finely chopped fresh chives

1 cup finely chopped fresh fenugreek leaves

⅓ cup vegetable oil, plus 3 tablespoons

1 medium yellow onion, finely chopped

1 pound lamb loin, cut into 1-inch cubes

1 teaspoon ground turmeric

5 cups water

1 cup kidney beans, soaked in water overnight

5 whole dried limes, soaked in water for 1 hour

1 teaspoon salt

1 teaspoon freshly ground black pepper

Chelo for serving

Preparation

Heat a large skillet over low heat, add the chives, parsley, cilantro, and fenugreek. Cook and stir frequently for about 11 minutes or until the herbs dry out a little. Add ⅓ cup of vegetable oil and cook the herbs, stirring constantly, for about 15 minutes more. Turn off the heat and set the herbs aside.

Heat the remaining 3 tablespoons of vegetable oil in a large pot over medium heat. When the oil begins to shimmer, add the onion and sauté until it's golden brown, about 10 minutes. Add the lamb and turmeric to the pot and sauté until the lamb is light brown on all sides, about 6 minutes. Add the water to the pot, increase the heat to high, bring the liquid to a boil, then reduce the heat to medium and simmer the stew for 9-11 minutes. Drain the kidney beans and add them to the stew. Cover the pot and simmer for 30 minutes; then add the sautéed herbs, cover the pot again, reduce the heat to low, and cook for 1 to 1½ hours.

Check on the stew every 30 minutes and add ½ cup more water if the stew seems too dry. Don't add too much water, though, as you want the end result to be thick and hearty. Drain the dried limes, prick them all over with a fork, and add them to the stew, along with the salt and pepper. Simmer for another 15 minutes to infuse the flavors.

Pomegranate and Walnut Stew

Preparation time: 10 minutes

Cook time: 120 minutes

Nutrition facts: Calories 557/ carbs 14 g/Fat 34g /Protein 50 g

Ingredients (4 servings)

1 pound shelled unsalted walnuts

1 tablespoon vegetable oil

1 medium yellow onion, finely chopped

3 cups warm water

1 pound cooked and mashed pumpkin

6 skinless, bone-in chicken thighs

1½ cups pomegranate molasses, divided

2 tablespoons brown sugar (optional)

1 teaspoon salt

½ teaspoon freshly ground black pepper

Chelo for serving

Preparation

Using a food processor, grind the walnuts into very fine crumbs. Set aside. Heat the vegetable oil in a large pot over medium heat. When the oil begins to shimmer, add the onion and sauté until it's golden brown, about 10 minutes. Add the crushed walnuts and cook for 6 minutes, stirring constantly, then pour in the water. Increase the heat to medium high, bring the liquid to a boil, then reduce the heat to medium, add the pumpkin and chicken, cover the pot. Simmer for 27-30 minutes or until the chicken is cooked through. Add 1 cup of pomegranate molasses, cover the pot, and simmer for an additional 15 minutes.

Take the chicken thighs out of the stew and place them on a plate. Set them aside. Taste the stew. If it's too sour for your taste, add the brown sugar; if it's not sour enough, add the remaining ½ cup of pomegranate molasses. Stir in the salt and pepper, then cover the pot and let the stew simmer for 30 more minutes. If the stew is too thick, add 1 extra cup of water. Add the chicken thighs back into the stew, cover the pot, and simmer for 18-22 minutes or until the chicken is heated through. Serve hot with *chelo*.

Green Bean Stew

Preparation time: 10 minutes

Cook time: 110 minutes

Nutrition facts: Calories 239/ carbs 25 g/Fat 12g /Protein 6 g

Ingredients (4 servings)

5 tablespoons vegetable oil, divided

2 medium yellow onions, finely chopped

1 pound lamb loin, cut into ½-inch cubes

1 teaspoon ground turmeric

3 cups water

1 pound fresh green beans, trimmed and cut into 2-inch pieces

1 teaspoon salt

1 teaspoon freshly ground black pepper

2 tablespoons bloomed saffron (optional, see here)

3 tablespoons tomato paste

4 tablespoons freshly squeezed lemon juice

1 large white potato, peeled and cut into small cubes

Preparation

Heat 2 tablespoons of vegetable oil in a large pot over medium heat. When the oil begins to shimmer, add the onions and sauté for 9-11 minutes or until golden brown. Add the lamb and cook 5-7 minutes or until the lamb pieces are light brown on all sides. Stir in the turmeric and mix well. Add the water to the pot, cover, and let the stew cook for 28-32 minutes or until the lamb is halfway cooked. The meat will be light brown but not completely tender. Add the green beans to the pot, cover, and cook for another 28-32 minutes or until both the beans and the lamb are tender. Check the stew occasionally to make sure there is enough water in the pot and add more, as needed. Stir in the salt, pepper, bloomed saffron and tomato paste. Stir until the tomato paste is completely dissolved in the stew, then add the lemon juice, cover the pot, and turn off the heat while you make the potatoes.

Heat the remaining 3 tablespoons of vegetable oil in a small saucepan over medium heat. When the oil begins to shimmer, add the potato and sauté until it is golden brown and tender, 15 to 22 minutes. Serve the stew hot with *chelo*, topped with the potatoes.

Zucchini Stew

Preparation time: 10 minutes
Cook time: 60 minutes
Nutrition facts: Calories 314/ carbs 42 g/Fat 8g /Protein 22 g

Ingredients (4 servings)

5 tablespoons vegetable oil, divided
4 zucchini, peeled and halved lengthwise, then cut into thin half-moons
6 skinless, bone-in chicken thighs
1 onion, finely chopped
1 teaspoon ground turmeric
½ teaspoon freshly ground black pepper
2 tablespoons tomato paste
2½ cups water
1 teaspoon salt
2 tablespoons freshly squeezed lemon juice
Chelo for serving

Preparation

Heat 2 tablespoons of vegetable oil in a large pot over medium heat. When the oil begins to shimmer, add the zucchini and cook for 6 to 8 minutes or just until golden. Transfer the zucchini to a plate and set it aside. In the same pot over medium heat, heat 2 tablespoons of vegetable oil. When the oil begins to shimmer, add the chicken thighs and cook 7 minutes or until they are browned on both sides. Transfer the chicken to a plate and set it aside. Heat the remaining 1 tablespoon of vegetable oil in the same pot over medium heat and sauté the onion until golden brown, about 10 minutes. Add the turmeric and black pepper. Stir well. Add the water and tomato paste and stir until the tomato paste is dissolved.

Increase the heat to medium high and bring the stew to a boil, then reduce the heat to medium and add the chicken thighs. Cover the pot and cook for 19-22 minutes or until the chicken thighs are completely cooked. Add the zucchini, salt, and lemon juice to the pot. Simmer uncovered for another 10 minutes or until the zucchini is heated through.

Serve with *chelo.*

Celery Stew

Preparation time: 15 minutes

Cook time: 110 minutes

Nutrition facts: Calories 261/ carbs 10 g/Fat 8g /Protein 16 g

Ingredients (4 servings)

4 tablespoons vegetable oil, divided

1½ cups finely chopped fresh parsley

1 cup finely chopped fresh mint

7 celery stalks, cut into ½-inch pieces

1 large yellow onion, finely chopped

1 pound beef loin, cut into ½-inch chunks

4 cups water

3 whole dried Persian limes

1 tablespoon bloomed saffron (see here)

1 teaspoon salt

1 teaspoon freshly ground black pepper

Chelo for serving

Preparation

Heat 2 tablespoons of vegetable oil in a large pot over medium heat. When the oil begins to simmer, add the parsley, mint, and celery and sauté for 3 minutes. Immediately transfer the herbs and celery to a plate and set aside. Heat the remaining 2 tablespoons of vegetable oil in the same pot over medium heat. When the oil begins to shimmer, add the onion and sauté until it's translucent, about 5 minutes; then add the beef and sauté for 4 minutes or until it's light brown on all sides.

Add the water and bring it to a boil, then reduce the heat to low, cover the pot, and let the stew simmer for 20-22 minutes. Add the sautéed herbs and celery.

Cover and simmer 45-55 minutes or until the meat is fully cooked and the celery is soft. Prick the dried limes all over with a fork, drop them in the stew, cover the pot, and cook for another 22-25 minutes to infuse the flavor. Stir in the bloomed saffron, salt, and pepper. Cover and cook for 10 minutes more. Serve hot with *chelo*.

Persian Lamb Stew

Preparation time: 200 minutes

Cook time: 50 minutes

Nutrition facts: Calories 368/ carbs 15 g/Fat 23g /Protein 0 g

Ingredients (4 servings)

2 cups of steamed basmati rice

1/8 cup of fresh parsley

1½ tablespoons of tomato paste

1½ pounds of chopped lamb

1 minced medium onion

1½ tablespoons of olive oil

½ teaspoons of pepper flakes, crushed

½ teaspoons of sea salt

1 teaspoon of ground pepper

½ tablespoons of turmeric

Preparation

Mix red pepper, salt, pepper, and turmeric in small bowl. Heat olive oil and onion on med high in large pot until it's hot but not yet smoking. Sauté for 12 minutes or until onion is golden brown and softened. Add the lamb meat to pot. Brown for several minutes on both sides. Drain all fat that may collect from the bottom of the pot. Evenly sprinkle seasonings across the top of lamb. Cover lamb with 4 cups of filtered water. Bring to slow boil. Reduce the heat to med-low and simmer for 110-130 minutes at that heat level. Skim the fat from the surface every ½ hour. Add the tomato paste to the pot. Stir until it dissolves in broth. Simmer for 20 more minutes without cover on pot, while stirring occasionally. Sauce should thicken and meat should be tender. Taste and adjust the seasoning, if needed. Garnish with parsley.

Traditional Persian Stew With Potato and Rice

Preparation time: 10 minutes
Cook time: 30 minutes
Nutrition facts: Calories 260/ carbs 46 g/Fat 6g /Protein 4 g

Ingredients (6 servings)
3 cups white long grain rice
¼ cup oil
4 potatoes
4 oz. water

Preparation
Place in it the rice in a larger bowl and cover it with hot water and a pinch of salt. Place it aside. Peel of the potato and slice them. Place a medium pot and fill ½ of it with water. Place in it the rice and cook it to boiling. Once the rice is half done, drain it.

Place a large pot over medium heat and heat the oil in it. Spread the potato in the pot and sprinkle on it some salt. Top it with rice. Make a hole in the center of the rice layer and another 4 holes on the side. Drizzle some water on top. Put on the lid and cook them for 3 min over high heat. Lower the heat and drizzle some oil top. Lower the heat to medium heat and cook it for 14-17 min and then further lower the heat to medium low. Drizzle more of some oil on top. Finally, cook it for 12 minutes and serve warm.

Cinnamon Beef Stew

Preparation time: 10 minutes

Cook time: 100 minutes

Nutrition facts: Calories 493/ carbs 5 g/Fat 34g /Protein 39 g

Ingredients

1 pound lean stew beef, cut into cubes

3 tablespoons olive oil, divided

1 cans kidney bean, drained and rinsed

2 teaspoon turmeric

½ onion, chopped

½ teaspoon cinnamon

6 tablespoons fresh parsley, chopped

2 ½ cups. water

3 tablespoon chives

1 lemon, juice of

2 teaspoon ground cumin

1 tablespoon flour

Salt and black pepper

Preparation

Place a large pan over medium heat. Heat 2 tablespoon of olive oil in it. Brown in it the stew meat for 12-14 minutes. Stir in the cumin, turmeric and cinnamon. Cook them for 2 minutes. Pour in the water and cook them until they start boiling. Put on the lid and cook them for 50-53 minutes while stirring from to time. Place a small skillet over medium heat and add 1 tablespoon of oil in it. Add the parsley with chives and cook for 3 min. Stir them into the beef stew with beans and lemon juice. Sprinkle some salt and pepper on the stew then add to it 1 tablespoon of flour. Cook the stew for 37 minutes or until it thickens and serve.

Potato Lamb Stew

Preparation time: 10 minutes

Cook time: 80 minutes

Nutrition facts: Calories 427/ carbs 21 g/Fat 28g /Protein 23 g

Ingredients (4 servings)

1 pound lamb, cut in cubes

¼ cups butter

1 pound green beans, cut in one-inch pieces

1 cup tomato paste

1 pound. carrot, cut in one-inch slices

2 large waxy potatoes, cut in one-inch cubes

½ teaspoon cinnamon

1 teaspoon salt

¼ teaspoon black pepper

1 teaspoon turmeric

Preparation

Season the lamb meat with cinnamon. Place a large pan over medium heat. Melt the butter in it. Cook the meat in it in batches for 4-5 minutes per batch. Stir in 2 cups of water and cook them until they start boiling. Lower the heat and cook them for 38-42 minutes with the lid on. Stir in the carrots, green beans, tomato paste, potatoes, and spices. Cook them for another 35-38 min with the lid on. Adjust the seasoning of the stew and then serve it warm.

Curry

Mushroom Tomato Curry

Preparation time: 10 minutes

Cook time: 13 minutes

Nutrition facts: Calories 577/ carbs 70 g/Fat 30g /Protein 17 g

Ingredients (2 servings)

1 cup tomatoes, diced

2 cups shiitake mushrooms, diced

2 tablespoon tomato puree

Fresh parsley, chopped

1 teaspoon red chili powder

½ teaspoon cumin

½ teaspoon coriander powder

4 garlic cloves, sliced

1 teaspoon oil

2 onions, sliced

1 cup mushroom stock

Yogurt to serve

Rice to serve

Preparation

In a pan, heat the oil and add the sliced garlic and onion. Cook for 2 minutes and add the cumin, tomato puree, coriander powder, salt, red chili powder, and mushroom stock. Bring it to a boil and simmer for 3 minutes. Add the shiitake mushrooms and diced tomatoes and cook for 6-8 minutes. Serve hot on rice and add parsley and yogurt on top.

Persian Vegetable Curry

Preparation time: 10 minutes

Cook time: 28 minutes

Nutrition facts: Calories 308/ carbs 39 g/Fat 11g /Protein 8 g

Ingredients (8 servings)

¼ cup + 2 tablespoons sweet potato

¼ cup + 2 tablespoons medium eggplant

¼ cup + 2 tablespoons green bell pepper

½ cup + 2 tablespoons carrots

¼ cup + 2 tablespoons from a can of garbanzo beans

1 tablespoon and 1 teaspoon almonds

¼ cup + 2 tablespoons onion

1 clove garlic

¼ cup + 2 tablespoons red bell pepper

¼ cup + 2 tablespoons zucchini

3 ½-ounces spinach

2 tablespoons olive oil

¾ teaspoon sea salt

¼ teaspoon ground turmeric

2 teaspoons raisins

1/3 cup orange juice

¼ teaspoon cayenne pepper

1 teaspoon curry powder

¼ teaspoon ground cinnamon

Preparation

In a large skillet, sauté the first potatoes, eggplants, bell papers, carrots, and onion with 2 tablespoons of oil. In a pot, mix the garlic, cinnamon, turmeric, olive oil, curry powder, pepper and salt. Then heat for 3 minutes. Combine the spice mixture with the garlic mixture and simmer with the remaining ingredients for about 20 minutes. Lastly, add the spinach leaves and cook for about 5-6 minutes. Serve with rice or bread.

Persian Bean Curry

Preparation time: 7 minutes

Cook time: 18 minutes

Nutrition facts: Calories 228/ carbs 39 g/Fat 4g /Protein 11 g

Ingredients (5 servings)

1 cup spinach

1 cup boiled kidney beans

1 cup bell pepper, sliced

Fresh parsley, chopped

1 teaspoon garlic paste

1 teaspoon butter

2 cups mushroom stock

Salt to taste

1 red chili

Preparation

In a large pot, add the kidney beans with garlic, stock, salt and cook for 10 minutes. Add the butter, spinach, parsley, red chili, butter, and bell pepper. Cook for 8 minutes. Serve hot with Persian bread.

Chickpea Lentil Spinach Curry

Preparation time: 5 minutes
Cook time: 20 minutes
Nutrition facts: Calories 204/ carbs 20 g/Fat 7g /Protein 11 g

Ingredients (4 servings)
1 cup boiled chickpeas
1 cup lentils
1 cup spinach, chopped
½ teaspoon turmeric
2 garlic cloves, minced
1 white onion, chopped
2 tablespoon butter
1-inch ginger, minced
½ teaspoon cumin
½ teaspoon cinnamon powder
½ teaspoon red chili powder
2 cups mushroom stock
Yogurt to serve
Salt and pepper to taste
Walnuts to serve

Preparation
In a large pot, add the butter, ginger, and garlic. Toss for 30 seconds and add the chopped onion. Toss for 1 minute and add the lentils. Stir for 3 minutes and pour in the stock. Cook for 9-11 minutes on high heat. Add the turmeric, red chili powder, salt, cinnamon and cumin before mixing well. Add the chickpeas and cook for 6 minutes. Add the spinach and cook for 6 minutes. Serve hot with walnuts, pepper, and yogurt on top.

Eggplant Tamarind Curry

Preparation time: 5 minutes

Cook time: 20 minutes

Nutrition facts: Calories 392/ carbs 63 g/Fat 9g /Protein 9 g

Ingredients (4 servings)

6 medium eggplants

1 cup tomatoes, chopped

2 tablespoon tamarind paste

1 teaspoon red chili powder

1 teaspoon cumin

¼ teaspoon cinnamon

1 tablespoon oil

1 tablespoon sugar

2 white onions, sliced

2 garlic cloves, sliced

Salt to taste

Fresh parsley, chopped

Preparation

Cut a few slits on the eggplants. In a pan, add the oil and fry the eggplants for 6 minutes. Transfer them on a plate. In the same pan, add the garlic and onion. Cook until golden brown. Add the tomato and toss for 2 minutes. Add the tamarind paste, cumin, red chili powder, cinnamon, and salt. Toss for 6 minutes. Add the eggplants again. Add the parsley and sugar. Lastly, cook for 3 minutes. Serve hot.

Persian Kofta Curry

Preparation time: 10 minutes

Cook time: 15 minutes

Nutrition facts: Calories 400/ carbs 47 g/Fat 19g /Protein 10 g

Ingredients (4 servings)

2 cups beef, minced

1 egg

1 tablespoon rice flour

1 cup onions, chopped

1 1/2 cups tomatoes, chopped

1 tablespoon rosemary, chopped

Fresh coriander, chopped

Fresh parsley, chopped

6 peppercorns

½ teaspoon cinnamon powder

2 tablespoon oil

1 cup beef stock

Salt and pepper to taste

Yogurt to serve

Pomegranate seeds to serve

Preparation

Combine the minced beef with rice flour, egg and salt, pepper. Mix well and create meatballs. Fry them golden brown with oil. Transfer onto a kitchen paper. In a large pan, heat the oil. Add the onion and then cook for 1 minute. Add the tomatoes and cook for 2 minutes. Add the stock, cinnamon, salt, pepper, and peppercorns. Next, cook for 5 minutes on high heat. Add the fried meatballs, parsley, coriander, rosemary, and cook for 5 minutes. Serve with more herbs, pomegranate seeds, and yogurt.

Chicken Pomegranate Curry

Preparation time: 10 minutes
Cook time: 20 minutes
Nutrition facts: Calories 390/ carbs 54 g/Fat 9 g /Protein 23 g

Ingredients (4 servings)

2 pound chicken, cut into pieces

1 cup pomegranate juice

Fresh parsley, chopped

1 teaspoon garlic paste

1 teaspoon red chili powder

1 teaspoon cumin

1 teaspoon ginger paste

1 tablespoon butter

¼ teaspoon saffron combined with 1 tablespoon warm milk

1 onion, chopped

1 cinnamon stick

1 cup chicken stock

Salt to taste

1 bay leaf

2 peppercorns

Pomegranate seeds to serve

Preparation

In a large pan, melt the butter and add the chicken. Sear it for 5 minutes and transfer to a plate. In the same pan, add the onion, ginger paste, garlic paste and toss for 1 minute. Add bay leaf, cinnamon stick, peppercorns, cumin, and red chili powder. Add the stock and cook on high heat for 5 minutes. Add the chicken again and cook for 6-7 minutes. Add salt, saffron mix, pomegranate juice, and herbs. Cook for 6 minutes. Remove from the heat and serve with fresh pomegranate seeds on top.

Soup

Persian Chicken Meatball Soup (*Gundi*)

Preparation time: 15 minutes

Cook time: 80 minutes

Nutrition facts: Calories 346/ carbs 0 g/Fat 27g /Protein 25 g

Ingredients (6 servings)

1 bay leaf

8 cups chicken stock

3 onions, 2 roughly chopped, 1 minced

¼ cup canola oil

1 ½ teaspoon baking soda

1 pound chicken wings

2 ½ teaspoon ground turmeric

½ teaspoon ground cardamom

1 ½ pounds ground chicken

3 carrots, chopped

2 cloves garlic, crushed

2 teaspoon ground coriander

1 ½ cups chickpea flour

Salt

Black pepper

Preparation

Pour 3 tablespoon oil in a pan and heat over medium heat. Salt and pepper the chicken wings to your taste and cook for 14-16 minutes, or until the color changes to brown. Add the carrots, chopped onions, and garlic and cook 10 minutes and stir occasionally. Add chicken stock, bay leaf, and salt. Boil until it starts to bubble. Reduce the heat and cook for 19-22 minutes. Strain the broth and get rid of the solids. Pour the broth back into the pan. Pour the unused oil in a 12-inch skillet and heat over medium heat. Add minced onion and cook for 4 minutes, or until soft. Pour into a bowl and add the remaining ingredients. Mix until they blend thoroughly. Wet your hands. Now, shape the mixture into six 3-inch balls. Go back to the broth and bring to a simmer. When done, add the meatballs and cook for 16- 22 minutes. Cover slightly. Serve broth and meatballs.

Whey Soup (*Kaleh Joosh*)

Preparation time: 10 minutes
Cook time: 20 minutes
Nutrition facts: Calories 76/ carbs 1.5 g/Fat 6.7g /Protein 2.5 g

Ingredients (2 servings)

1 onion, diced

2 cups (*Kashk*) whey

1 cup walnut

2 tablespoon chopped mint

1 tablespoon black pepper

½ teaspoon salt

2 garlic cloves

1 tablespoon turmeric

Water

Oil

Preparation

Pour oil inside pot and heat over medium heat. Put onions inside and sauté until they change to golden. Grind the garlic cloves and put inside the pot. Add salt, pepper, turmeric, and mix well. Add mint into the mixture and stir. Break the walnuts and mince. Now, put in the pot and fry with the other content. Pour whey into the pot and mix thoroughly until it blends with the other ingredients. If the paste is too thick, add boiling water. Pour a cup of water. Leave it to simmer for 16-20 minutes over low heat.

Eggplant Soup

Preparation time: 10 minutes

Cook time: 15 minutes

Nutrition facts: Calories 119/ carbs 23 g/Fat 3g /Protein 3 g

Ingredients (4 servings)

1 cup spinach puree

4 large eggplants

½ cup onions, sliced

1 cup heavy cream

1 green chili

1 teaspoon honey

1 teaspoon lemon juice

Fresh coriander, chopped

Yogurt to serve

Oil for frying

Salt and pepper to taste

Preparation

In a grilling pan, add the oil and roast the eggplants for 5-6 minutes. Transfer them into a bowl. Remove the skin. Use your hands to mash it finely. In a pot, heat 1 tablespoon of oil and caramelize the onion. Transfer the onion onto a plate. Add the mashed eggplant, green chili, salt, pepper, coriander, spinach puree, and cook for 5 minutes. Add the cream and honey. Cook for 5 minutes. Serve hot with spinach puree, pepper, and yogurt.

Persian Noodle Soup

Preparation time: 15 minutes

Cook time: 80 minutes

Nutrition facts: Calories 255/ carbs 31 g/Fat 11g /Protein 10 g

Ingredients (6 servings)

8 ounces linguine, dried, cooked

8 ounces spinach, chopped

6 cups water

1 cup parsley leaves, chopped

½ cup navy beans, dried

½ cup sunflower oil

½ cup scallions, chopped

¼ cup mint, dried

¼ cup brown lentils

¼ cup fava beans, dried

Salt, to taste

Fresh ground black pepper, to taste

½ yellow onion, sliced

Preparation

Add navy beans lentils, fava beans, and water in a saucepan. Place over high heat and bring the mixture to the boil. Turn heat to a gentle simmer and let simmer covered for about 60 minutes. Add half of the oil in a saucepan and heat over medium. When hot, add mint and cook for 30 seconds. Take off heat and keep for later use. Add reserved oil in a skillet and heat over medium-high. Cook onions and turmeric for 9-12 minutes. Take off heat and pour onions and turmeric into a bowl, keep for serving. Add scallions, spinach, and parsley to beans, cover, and cook for 15 minutes. Add salt and pepper, and mint and oil. Add pasta, heat through, and take off heat. Serve garnished with yogurt and fried onions.

Barley Soup

Preparation time: 15 minutes
Cook time: 100 minutes
Nutrition facts: Calories 110/ carbs 25 g/Fat 11g /Protein 21 g

Ingredients (8 servings)

1 cup pearl barley

1 cup carrots, sliced

¼ cup tomato paste

½ cup parsley, fresh, chopped

½ cup sour cream

2 quarts hot chicken stock

8 lime wedges, for garnish

Freshly squeezed juice from 1 lime

Salt and pepper, to taste

1 onion, sliced

1 teaspoon turmeric

2 tablespoons vegetable oil

Preparation

In a large stock pot, add oil, and heat over medium. Add onions and cook 6 minutes or until tender. Stir in lime juice, barley, tomato paste, turmeric, and chicken stock. Season to taste with salt and pepper. Bring to the boil and lower heat to a gentle simmer and let simmer for 55-65 minutes. Add carrots, stir gently, and simmer for another 35 minutes. Stir in sour cream, mix to combine well. Add parsley and then mix well. Garnish with lime wedges and serve.

New Year's Bean Soup

Preparation time: 15 minutes
Cook time: 160 minutes
Nutrition facts: Calories 129/ carbs 22 g/Fat 2 g /Protein 13 g

Ingredients (6 servings)

3 yellow onions, diced
5 garlic cloves, minced
1 bunch leafy greens, chopped
1 handful mint leaves, fresh, chopped
½ cup parsley, fresh
½ cup cilantro, fresh, minced
¼ cup dill leaves, fresh, minced
¼ cup kidney beans, soaked overnight
¼ cup lentils, dried
½ cup chickpeas, soaked overnight
½ cup fava beans, soaked overnight
2 cups plain yogurt
6 ounces linguine, broken
1 teaspoon turmeric, ground
7 tablespoons olive oil, divided
Salt, to taste

Preparation

Add 4 tablespoons of oil in a large stock pot and heat over medium-high. Add ½ of the onions and cook for 5 minutes or until tender. Add half of the garlic and turmeric and cook for 30 seconds. Place in the kidney beans, lentils, fava beans, chickpeas, and vegetable stock. Bring the mixture to the boil. Cover and let boil for 55-65 minutes. Reduce heat to a simmer. Let simmer partially covered for 95-100 minutes. Taste and season with salt if needed. Add reserved oil in a skillet and heat over high. Cook reserved onions until browned, about 5 minutes. Sprinkle with salt and take off heat. Keep aside for serving. In the stock pot, add noodles and cook for 8 minutes or until al dente. Add leafy greens, parsley, cilantro, and dill. Heat through and serve topped with fried onions and yogurt.

Persian Lentil Soup

Preparation time: 10 minutes
Cook time: 60 minutes
Nutrition facts: Calories 240/ carbs 40 g/Fat 1g /Protein 18 g

Ingredients (8 servings)

8 cups vegetable stock

1 cup lentils

15 ounces can stew tomatoes

1 bunch parsley, fresh, chopped

4 garlic cloves, minced

1 onion, chopped

¼ teaspoon cayenne

½ teaspoon pepper

½ teaspoon salt

1 tablespoon olive oil

3 teaspoons 7-spice

Freshly squeezed juice from 1 lemon

Preparation

In a large stock pot, add oil and heat over medium. When hot, add garlic and onions and cook until translucent. Mix in lentils and vegetable stock and bring to the boil. Lower the heat to a simmer and let it simmer covered for 26-28 minutes. Mix in the parsley, tomatoes, cayenne, pepper, 7-spice, and salt. Continue simmering for 4-7 minutes. Reduce the heat and cook for 30 minutes. Stir in the lemon juice. Taste and season as desired.

Beet Soup

Preparation time: 20 minutes

Cook time: 55 minutes

Nutrition facts: Calories 229/ carbs 17 g/Fat 16g /Protein 5 g

Ingredients (6 servings)

3 cups water, filtered

1 grated onion

1 pound of ground turkey

1 teaspoon of pomegranate paste

2 fresh pomegranates, juice only

1 bunch red beets, including roots and leaves

Turmeric

Salt & ground black pepper

Preparation

Chop beets leaves and roots into cubes. Add water and cook in a large pot for 25 to 35 minutes over medium heat, with the pot covered. Add pomegranate paste and juice and stir. Add salt and pepper and cover the pot again. Prepare meat balls while soup simmers and cooks. Mix ground turkey, turmeric, and onion in a medium bowl. Remove lid from soup pot. Form small meatballs and add carefully to soup. Allow soup and meatballs to cook for 35 minutes longer and then serve.

Persian Chicken Soup

Preparation time: 10 minutes

Cook time: 120 minutes

Nutrition facts: Calories 166/ carbs 16 g/Fat 6 g /Protein 10 g

Ingredients (4 servings)

1 tablespoon of canola oil

2 limes, Persian, dried

2 chopped zucchinis

1 potato

1 large onion, yellow

1 tablespoon of ground turmeric

2 chicken thighs

Sea salt and ground pepper

Preparation

Heat canola oil in a large pot on medium heat. Dice the onion and add with turmeric to the pot. Cook for 3-4 minutes or until the onion is translucent. Cut the potato and zucchini into chunks and drop into the pot. Add limes and chicken, as well as salt and pepper, to taste.

Cover the pot contents with water. Bring to a boil on high heat. Once the ingredients are boiling, lower burner to lowest setting. Allow to simmer for 110-130 minutes or until veggies are cooked all the way through and chicken is so tender that it falls off the bones. Serve hot.

Yogurt Soup

Preparation time: 10 minutes

Nutrition facts: Calories 315/ carbs 37 g/Fat 12 g /Protein 19 g

Ingredients (6 servings)

32 oz. fluid plain yogurt

½ cups kefir cheese

1 large cucumber

2 tablespoons mint, dried and crushed

2 tablespoons basil, fresh finely chopped

1 teaspoon onion powder

2 tablespoons dried rose petals

½ cups walnuts, crushed

½ cups raisins

Salt and black pepper, to taste

Preparation

In a large mixing bowl combine the yogurt and kefir cheese and mix well. Peel the cucumbers and chop them finely. Stir in the pepper, mint, basil, onion powder, salt, walnuts, raisins and dried rose petals. Place it in the fridge until ready to serve.

Veggie Orange Soup

Preparation time: 15 minutes

Cook time: 50 minutes

Nutrition facts: Calories 25/ carbs 2 g/Fat 0 g /Protein 0 g

Ingredients (6 servings)

1 cup pistachios, shelled

1 -2 tablespoon olive oil

1 shallot, diced finely

1 leek, chopped finely

1 garlic clove, minced

3 tablespoons rice flour

1 teaspoon salt

¼ teaspoon pepper

¼ cups orange juice

6 cups of chicken broth or stock

2 tablespoon lime juice or 2 tablespoon lemon juice

2 tablespoon pistachios, slivered (for garnish)

Preparation

Rinse the pistachios and soak them for several minutes. Transfer them to a food processor and process them until they become smooth. Place a large saucepan over medium heat. Heat the oil in it. Add the shallot, leek and the garlic and cook t for 3-5 minutes. Stir in the rice flour. Pour in the broth while stirring. Cook them until they start boiling. Stir in the ground pistachios, salt, and pepper. Lower the heat, put on the lid and cook for 48-55 minutes. Add the orange and lemon juices. Adjust the seasoning and then serve it warm.

Yogurt Beef Soup

Preparation time: 10 minutes

Cook time: 110 minutes

Nutrition facts: Calories 169/ carbs 15 g/Fat 8g /Protein 9 g

Ingredients (6 servings)

2 pounds ground beef

2 eggs

½ cups fresh parsley, chopped

4 cups fresh spinach

1 onion, finely chopped

1 small onion, grated

¼ cups lentils

¼ cups kidney bean

1-quart plain yogurt

1 cup uncooked rice

½ teaspoon turmeric, for color

1 dash salt

1 dash pepper

1-quart water

Preparation

In a mixing bowl whisk in it the turmeric, salt, pepper, and yogurt and then put it in the fridge. Place a large pan over medium heat and heat a splash of oil in it. Add the onion and cook it for 4-6 minutes. Stir in the parsley, spinach, beans, and water while adding more to cover them, if needed. Cook them for 70 minutes.

In a large mixing bowl combine beef, eggs, dash of salt and pepper, and grated onion and mix them well. Shape the mix into meatballs and stir the rice with meatballs into the soup. Cook them for 32-35 minutes. Place the soup aside to lose heat for 16-20 minutes. Take some liquid from the soup and add it to the yogurt mix. Whisk it well until it becomes smooth. Stir the mix into the soup. Adjust the seasoning of the soup and then serve it warm.

Persian Pomegranate Soup (*Ash-e Anar*)

Preparation time: 10 minutes

Cook time: 55 minutes

Nutrition facts: Calories 451/ Fats 22.5 g/ Carbs 45.4 g/ Proteins 19.1 g

Ingredients (8 servings)

Broth

2 chopped large sweet onions

4 tablespoons olive oil

6 minced cloves garlic

2 quarts chicken stock

¾ cup yellow split peas

1 tablespoon ground turmeric

2 tablespoons ground black pepper

¾ teaspoon cayenne pepper

2 ¼ teaspoons mild paprika

1 cinnamon stick

¼ teaspoon ground fennel seeds

Meatballs

¼ cup minced onion

1 ½ pounds ground lamb

2 tablespoons minced fresh mint

1 minced clove garlic

2 tablespoons minced fresh parsley

½ cup minced fresh parsley

1 tablespoon honey

½ cup minced fresh mint

¼ cup pomegranate molasses

1 cup basmati rice

Garnish

¼ cup heavy whipping cream

2 cups pomegranate seeds

Preparation

In a heavy stockpot, heat the oil to moderately high heat. Stir-fry the onions for 4-6 minutes or until translucent. Sauté the garlic for 2-3 minutes until browned. Add the split peas and cook for 1 minute until the color changes. Pour the chicken stock; add the turmeric, paprika, pepper, cayenne, cinnamon stick and fennel seeds. Boil the soup and simmer on low heat for 22-24 minutes or until the split peas are tender. Meanwhile, combine the lamb meat, minced onion, parsley, garlic, and mint form in a bowl into meatballs as big as the size of walnuts. Drop the meatballs into the soup mixture and cook for 11-13 minutes until the center of the meat is no longer pinkish in color. Remove and discard the cinnamon stick. Stir in honey, basmati rice, pomegranate molasses, parsley, and mint to the mixture. Cook for 22-24 minutes until the rice is soft. Fill individual bowls with the soup and garnish on top with whipping cream and pomegranate seeds.

Chickpea and Coconut Soup

Preparation time: 15 minutes
Cook time: 35 minutes
Nutrition facts: Calories 189/ carbs 24 g/Fat 10g /Protein 3 g

Ingredients (5 servings)

2 apples
3 cups light vegetable broth
1 yellow bell pepper
1 can fire roasted diced tomatoes
1 can of coconut milk
4 cloves garlic
½ cup roasted green chilis
1 large sweet potato
Ground pepper
A pinch of cumin
1 cup baby greens
Juice of 1 lime
2 tablespoons chopped fresh cilantro
1 tablespoon curry paste
Pinch of cinnamon
1 can of chickpeas
Pepper flakes to taste

Preparation

In a slow cooker, add all the ingredients and cook on low heat for about 32 minutes. Simmer for 5-7 more minutes before serving in individual bowls. Eat with a side-dish of whole-grain bread sticks.

Salads

Persian Salad with Brown Rice and Cucumber

Preparation time: 40 minutes

Cook time: 20 minutes

Nutrition facts: Calories 523/ carbs 64 g/Fat 2.9g /Protein 11.8g

Ingredients (3 servings)

1 cup brown rice

Plenty water for soaking

2 cups water, for cooking the rice

1 teaspoon of salt

1 large cucumber, washed

½ cup pine nuts

1 small red onion

2 tablespoons olive oil

A bunch of baby spinach leaves

Juice of half a lemon

1 teaspoon honey

½ teaspoon cumin seeds

1 small garlic clove

A handful cilantro leaves

Salt and pepper, to taste

Preparation

Clean the rice and transfer to a large bowl to wash. Always stir gently to make sure you don't break the long rice grains. Drain and repeat until the water runs clear. Add ¼ teaspoon of salt to the soaking rice and leave uncovered for 35 minutes. Bring the rest of the salt and 2 cups of water to a boil. Drain the soaking rice and add to the boiling water. Cooking over medium heat until almost all the water has evaporated. Cover with a lid and lower the heat. Allow the rice to cook further for 5-6 minutes. Meanwhile, without peeling the cucumber, chop it into ¼-inch thick cubes. Wash the spinach leaves. Dice the red onion into very small pieces. Finely slice the cilantro leaves. Set aside.

Remove the rice from the heat and scatter on a tray to cool completely. In another bowl, whisk together the olive oil, honey, cumin, lemon juice, cilantro, salt, and pepper to create the salad dressing. Grate the garlic clove into the dressing. Add the diced onion and let it rest for 5-6 minutes. Once the rice is cool, mix it with the cucumber slices, spinach, and pine nuts. Drizzle the dressing on top and mix well to combine. Chill in the fridge for an hour before serving. Garnish with more cilantro leaves.

Chicken Salad

Preparation time: 10 minutes

Cook time: 30 minutes

Nutrition facts: Calories 370/ carbs 1 g/Fat 33g /Protein 14 g

Ingredients (4 servings)

1 1/3 pounds chicken breast halves, boneless, skinless, cut into bite size pieces

1 ½ pounds new potatoes, quartered

½ cup black olives, halved, pits removed

1 cup petite peas, frozen

½ cup basil, fresh, chopped

1/3 cup flat leaf parsley, chopped

¼ cup fresh lime juice

½ cup mayonnaise

1 cup plain yogurt

1 red onion, chopped

4 carrots, finely chopped

2 celery ribs, chopped

2 cucumbers, peeled, seeds removed, diced

1 ½ teaspoon black pepper, freshly ground

1 ½ teaspoons salt

1 tablespoon mustard

3 tablespoons olive oil

Preparation

Cook the potatoes in a pot of lightly salted water until tender. Drain and set aside. Add oil in a skillet and heat over medium. Rub the chicken with salt and pepper and cook in hot oil for 11-13 minutes or until evenly browned and well cooked. Meanwhile, add the lime juice, mayonnaise, mustard, and yogurt in a large bowl. Season with salt and pepper and whisk until well blended. Add all remaining ingredients. Toss to coat well and serve.

Cucumber and Tomato Salad

Preparation time: 15 minutes

Nutrition facts: Calories 60/ carbs 12 g/Fat 8g /Protein 2 g

Ingredients (4 servings)

3 Persian cucumbers or any seedless cucumbers, finely chopped

1 small red onion, finely chopped

2 large tomatoes, finely chopped

4 tablespoons lemon juice, freshly squeezed

½ teaspoon salt

½ teaspoon black pepper, freshly ground

1 tablespoon dried mint

Preparation

In a large bowl, mix the cucumbers, tomatoes, onion, pepper, salt and lemon juice. Cover the bowl and refrigerate the salad for 27-33 minutes. To serve, use dried mint to top and give it a nice stir.

Cabbage Salad

Preparation time: 25 minutes

Cook time: 20 minutes

Nutrition facts: Calories 225/ carbs 15 g/Fat 19g /Protein 2 g

Ingredients (5 servings)

3 tablespoons parsley, tarragon and basil

¼ red cabbage, large

2 tablespoons olive oil

1 pound tomatoes, grape

½ pound jicama (Mexican turnip)

1/8 teaspoons black pepper, cracked

¼ teaspoons salt

1 tablespoon oregano leaves, crushed

3 tablespoons olive oil

Sea salt, as desired

Black pepper, as desired

Preparation

Preheat the oven to 400 F. Wash and then pat grape tomatoes dry. Add to a large baking sheet lined with foil. Drizzle using 2 tablespoons of olive oil. Sprinkle with herbs, salt, and pepper. Toss the tomatoes and coat them completely and bake in oven for 22-25 minutes. While baking, watch for the tomatoes to burst and caramelize. Reset the oven to broil. Continue to cook for 2-3 more minutes, so that tomatoes become barely charred. Wash red cabbage leaves and cut into quarters. Slice the first quarter of cabbage into shreds. Add to a bowl for serving. Cut the jicama into halves. Save one to use later. Peel other half and slice into thin discs, then into shapes like French fries. Add to serving bowl. Add warm, charred tomatoes, herbs, olive oil, salt, and cracked pepper. Toss and serve as side salad or with toasted bread.

Cucumber and Peach Salad

Preparation time: 15 minutes

Nutrition facts: Calories 213/ carbs 34 g/Fat 5g /Protein 4 g

Ingredients (6 servings)

¼ cup of parsley, chopped

2 cups of fresh peaches

1 diced red pepper

2 cups of diced cucumber

Preparation

Combine red pepper and cucumbers in large bowl. Add cilantro and peach chunks gently and serve chilled.

Shiraz Salad

Preparation time: 15 minutes

Nutrition facts: Calories 144/ carbs 0 g/Fat 0 g /Protein 0 g

Ingredients (6 servings)

2 tablespoons of olive oil

¼ cup of lemon juice

Parsley

1 large onion

1 large tomato

1 large cucumber

Sea salt

Preparation

Chop cucumber, onion, and tomato into chunks, bite sized. To prepare the dressing, squeeze a large lemon and add olive oil and parsley to lemon juice. Whisk together and pour the dressing over the veggies. Add salt to taste and serve.

Persian Melon Salad

Preparation time: 10 minutes
Nutrition facts: Calories 194/ Fat 0.9 g/ Carbs 49 g/ Proteins 3 g

Ingredients (12 servings)

¼ watermelon

1 honeydew melon

1 bunch grapes

1 cantaloupe

1 pineapple

1 cup fresh orange juice

2 tablespoons pickled ginger

1 tablespoon white sugar

¼ cup chopped fresh mint

1-pint fresh hulled strawberries

¼ cup fresh lime juice

4 sprigs fresh mint

Preparation

Remove the pulp from cantaloupe, honeydew melon, and watermelon with a melon baller. Set aside. Peel and core the pineapple and cut into chunks, and then set aside. Combine the orange juice, watermelon, honeydew, grapes, cantaloupe, pineapple, pickled ginger, lime juice, mint and sugar in a large mixing bowl. Toss to combine well and cover the bowl and chill for one hour. Fold strawberries into the fruit mixture and garnish with mint sprigs before serving.

Sirloin Gyro Salad

Preparation time: 25 minutes

Cook time: 20 minutes

Nutrition facts: Calories 593/ carbs 74 g/Fat 12 g /Protein 44 g

Ingredients (4 servings)

8 cups mixed salad greens

2 ¼ teaspoons Persian *advieh* seasoning (store-bought)

½ cup plain yogurt

1 pound sirloin steak

1 small red onion

1 large tomato

½ cup sour cream

1 tablespoon olive oil

1 medium cucumber

¼ cup milk

Pita bread

Preparation

In a small bowl, mix milk, yogurt, sour cream, and 1 teaspoon *advieh* seasoning until creamy. Set aside. In a skillet, heat the oil, add beef and sprinkle with 1 ½ teaspoon *advieh* seasoning. When the beef turned golden brown, remove from the skillet. Meanwhile, prepare the toppings by dividing the mixed salad greens into individual plates; top with onions, tomatoes, and cucumber. Warm the pita bread in the skillet and slice into quarters. Place the beef inside the pita pockets and serve the salad on the side.

Arugula Salad (*Jarjeer*)

Preparation time: 15 minutes

Nutrition facts: Calories 450/ carbs 24 g/Fat 36g /Protein 13 g

Ingredients (4 servings)

1 bunch arugula

¼ cup chopped shallots

1 cup chopped mushrooms

1 teaspoon extra virgin olive oil

½ lemon, juiced

2 teaspoons sumac

Salt to taste

¼ cup chopped walnuts

Preparation

Wash the arugula thoroughly. Arrange the arugula, shallots, and mushrooms on a platter. Wisk together the olive oil, lemon juice, and sumac. Season the salad with salt and drizzle with the dressing. Sprinkle with chopped walnuts.

Glazed Lamb Salad With Fruits

Preparation time: 20 minutes

Cook time: 250 minutes

Nutrition facts: Calories 95.5/ carbs 14.4 g/Fat 4.8 g /Protein 1.4 g

Ingredients (6 servings)

4 tablespoon molasses, pomegranate

1 teaspoon ground cumin

Lemon juice

1 tablespoon olive oil

2 garlic cloves, minced

1 onion, roughly chopped

1 lamb shoulder

2 pomegranates, seeds only

A handful flat leaf parsley

100 g watercress

1 small red onion, finely diced

1 tablespoon olive oil

Flat bread, to serve

Preparation

Preheat the oven to 320 F. In a small mixing bowl stir in the molasses, garlic, lemon juice, cumin, and olive oil to make the sauce. Spread the onion in a greased casserole dish. Place the lamb on it and pour the ¾ sauce all over it. Add a piece of foil over the casserole dish. Cook it in the oven for 210-225 minutes. Toss the red onion with pomegranate and olive oil in a large salad bowl. Serve it with the roasted lamb warm.

Desserts

Saffron Rice Cake (*Tahchin-e Goosht*)

Preparation time: 10 minutes
Cook time: 165 minutes
Nutrition facts: Calories 432/ carbs 25 g/Fat 12g /Protein 30g

Ingredients (4 servings)

½ teaspoon saffron

1 pound chicken thighs

2 tablespoons olive oil

1 teaspoon turmeric

¼ teaspoon peppercorns

1 ¼ cup basmati rice

1 teaspoon olive oil

1 tablespoon melted butter

½ cup plain yogurt

2 egg yolks

1 teaspoon lemon juice

1 chopped onion

3 teaspoons sugar

3 garlic cloves

¼ cup diced or ground pistachios

¼ cup canola oil

2 tablespoons butter

Salt and pepper to taste

Preparation

Dissolved the saffron in 3 tablespoon water. Set aside in a warm place. Cube the chicken into edible pieces. Heat the oil and fry the chicken in a skillet on low for 9-11 minutes. Use the same skillet the fry the onion and garlic for 5 minutes. Stir the chicken, turmeric, and black peppercorn into the skillet and pour in 1 cup of boiling water. Simmer for 60 minutes and season with salt and pepper. Set aside.

Rinse the rice. Boil 12 cups of water and stir in the rice with a bit of salt. Cook for 9 minutes or until done. Stir in the saffron and 1/8 teaspoon salt. Combine the egg yolk and yogurt with 1/3 of the rice mixture. Spread the mixture on the bottom of a baking dish. Stir together the remaining rice and chicken mixture and place on top. Bake for 65-80 minutes and serve.

Sweet Rice Pudding with Rosewater and Cardamom (Sheer Berenj)

Preparation time: 50 minutes
Cook time: 130 minutes
Nutrition facts: Calories 419/ carbs 18 g/Fat 11.2g /Protein 18g

Ingredients (6 servings)

2 cups of long grain rice

Plenty of water to soak the rice

1 cup of sugar

¼ cup of honey

4 cups of water to cook rice

6 cups of milk

1 cup of cream

½ cup of rose water

¼ teaspoon of cinnamon powder

¼ teaspoon of ground cardamom seeds

Pistachios to garnish

Preparation

Clean the rice and transfer to a large bowl to wash. Add plenty to tap water to the bowl to submerge the rice in water. Using your hand and with light movements, stir the rice in the bowl to release the dirt. You'll notice the water will have turned murky. Drain and repeat step 1, until the water runs clear. Add ¼ teaspoon of salt to the soaking rice and leave uncovered for an hour or preferably overnight. Drain the water from the rice and set aside.

Bring 4 cups of water to a boil and add the drained rice to it. Cook, stirring constantly, until half the rice is still submerged in water. By this time, water will be very starchy. Simultaneously in another pot, bring the milk, cream, rose water, cinnamon powder, and cardamom powder to a slow boil.

When the milk has warmed, pour it into the cooking rice in slow streams while constantly stirring. Once all the milk has been added, cook the rice gently on low heat while stirring. When the milk has reduced to half, add the honey and sugar. Cook for another 20 minutes and turn off the heat. Allow the rice pudding to cool for a while before pouring into a dish. Chill for at least 130 minutes or overnight in the fridge. Decorate with dried figs or pistachios, just before serving.

Sweet Persian Rice Pudding Cooked With Saffron (*Sholeh Zard*)

Preparation time: 60 minutes

Cook time: 130 minutes

Nutrition facts: Calories 425/ Carbs 43 g/Fat 19g /Protein 28g

Ingredients (4 servings)

2 cups of starchy rice

6 cups of water for cooking the pudding

1 ½ cups granulated sugar

¼ teaspoon saffron powder

¼ cup of warm water

¼ teaspoon ground cardamom seeds

¼ teaspoon cinnamon powder

¼ cup good quality rose water

Plenty cinnamon to decorate

Plenty of water for soaking the rice

Slivered pistachios or pesteh, to garnish

Slivered almonds, to garnish

Preparation

Clean the rice and transfer to a large bowl to wash. Add plenty of tap water to the bowl to submerge the rice in water. Using your hand and with light movements, stir the rice in the bowl to release the dirt. Once the water becomes murky, drain and repeat until the water runs clear. Add ¼ teaspoon of salt to the soaking rice and leave uncovered for an hour or preferably overnight. Drain the water from the rice and set aside. Mix saffron powder with the warm water in a bowl; set aside.

Bring 6 cups of water to a boil and add the drained rice to it. Cook, stirring constantly, until half the rice is still submerged in water. By this time, water will be very starchy. Mix in the sugar, saffron water, rose water, cinnamon powder, and cardamom seeds. Mix well using a kafgir.

Lower the heat and cook the pudding using a kafgir until the sugar has dissolved and you're left with a thick yellow colored rice pudding. Take out into a dish and chill for at least two hours to let the pudding set. Create your innovative design on the pudding using cinnamon powder, almonds, and pistachios. Serve immediately.

Rice Flour Pudding

Preparation time: 5 minutes
Cook time: 25 minutes
Nutrition facts: Calories 352/ carbs 20 g/Fat 9 g /Protein 22 g

Ingredients (4 servings)

2 cups whole milk
½ cup water
4 tablespoons sugar
3 tablespoons rice flour
1 tablespoon rosewater

Preparation

Pour the milk, water, and sugar into a small saucepan and place it over medium heat. Stir for 5-7 minutes or until the mixture is warm and the sugar is completely dissolved. Turn off the heat. Using a ladle, pour ½ cup of the milk and water mixture into a bowl and add the rice flour to it. Whisk the flour into the liquid, making sure there are no lumps. Add the rice flour mixture to the pan and turn the heat back to medium. Stir constantly for 16 to 22 minutes or until the pudding is thick and well blended. Stir in the rosewater and cook for 1 minute more. Pour the pudding into small individual bowls and serve.

Rice Pudding (*Shir Berenj*)

Preparation time: 10 minutes
Cook time: 95 minutes
Nutrition facts: Calories 106/ carbs 19 g/Fat 2 g /Protein 4 g

Ingredients (4 servings)

1 cup short-grain white rice, soaked in water overnight

2 cups water

4 cups whole milk, at room temperature

½ cup sugar

3 tablespoons rosewater

1 teaspoon ground cardamom

Preparation

Drain the rice and add to a large pot with the water over medium heat. Bring the water to a boil, reduce the heat to low. Simmer for 28-32 minutes, half-covered, until the rice is almost tender. Gradually stir in the milk and sugar and continue cooking, uncovered for 38-42 minutes or until the rice is very soft. Stir the pudding occasionally while it's cooking to prevent it from sticking to the bottom of the pot. Add the rosewater and ground cardamom, stir, and cook for 9-11 minutes more. Turn off the heat, cover the pot, and let it sit for another 15 minutes. Spoon the pudding into small individual bowls and refrigerate until chilled.

Coconut Sweets

Preparation time: 15 minutes
Cook time: 15 minutes
Nutrition facts: Calories 383/ carbs 46 g/Fat 18g /Protein 9 g

Ingredients (8 servings)

1 cup sugar
½ cup water
¼ cup rosewater
2½ cups unsweetened shredded coconut, plus 2 tablespoons
Ground unsalted pistachios (optional)

Preparation

Mix the sugar and water in a medium saucepan and place it over medium heat. Cook 5-6 minutes or until the sugar is melted and dissolved and then stir in the rosewater. Cook for another 9-11 minutes or until the syrup starts to thicken. Turn off the heat and let the syrup cool for 15 minutes. Using a wire whisk, beat the syrup for 2-3 minutes. Place 2½ cups of shredded coconut in a large bowl and pour the syrup over the coconut. Using a wooden spoon, stir everything together until the mixture resembles a soft dough. Sprinkle the remaining 2 tablespoons of shredded coconut on the bottom of an 8-by-8-inch glass baking dish and spread the coconut dough over it. Cover and chill in the refrigerator for 3 hours before serving. To serve, cut the sweets into diamonds and top with ground pistachios, to taste.

Date Dessert

Preparation time: 20 minutes

Cook time: 10 minutes

Nutrition facts: Calories 25/ carbs 5 g/Fat 14 g /Protein 1 g

Ingredients (6 servings)

30 Medjool dates, pitted

1 cup whole, unsalted shelled walnuts

2 sticks unsalted butter

2 cups all-purpose flour

1 teaspoon ground cinnamon

1 teaspoon ground cardamom

2 tablespoons powdered sugar

Preparation

Stuff all the dates with walnuts, putting them in the cavity where the pit was, but don't to break the dates. Place them in a single layer in a pie plate or other shallow dish; set aside. Melt the butter in a small saucepan over medium heat and sift in the flour. Using a wooden spoon, stir constantly for 7-9 minutes or until the mixture turns golden brown and then stir in the cardamom and cinnamon. Remove the pan from the heat and set it aside. Let the mixture cool for 7 to 11 minutes. Pour the flour and butter mixture over the dates, making sure it covers the dates. Place in the refrigerator for 130 minutes or until the top is set. Sprinkle the powdered sugar and serve cold.

Honey Candy

Preparation time: 10 minutes

Cook time: 10 minutes

Nutrition facts: Calories 20/ carbs 5 g/Fat 0 g /Protein 0 g

Calories: 20 /Carbs: 5g /Fat: 0g /Protein: 0g

Ingredients (6 servings)

½ cup sugar

1 tablespoon honey

2 tablespoons vegetable oil

1 teaspoon bloomed saffron

½ cup mixed unsalted nuts

Preparation

Line two baking sheets with parchment paper; set aside. Put the honey, sugar and vegetable oil in a small saucepan. Cook for 5-7 minutes over medium heat, stirring, until the sugar starts to caramelize. Tilt the saucepan so the sugar melts evenly. When the sugar is completely melted and the mixture begins to simmer, lower the heat and add the bloomed saffron and nuts. Stir a couple of times so everything is fully combined, but don't stir the candy mixture too much, or the oil will separate from the sugar. Test the readiness of the candy by dropping a little bit of it into cold water. If it hardens into a crispy ball, it's ready. The color should be deep golden brown. Turn off the heat. Using a small spoon, quickly drop the candies onto the parchment paper in spoonsful. It should be quite quick, since the mixture will swiftly start to harden. Cool at room temperature for 20 minutes before serving.

Soft Rosewater Candy

Preparation time: 15 minutes
Cook time: 15 minutes
Nutrition facts: Calories 60/ carbs 15 g/Fat 0 g /Protein 0 g

Ingredients (8 servings)

1½ cups wheat starch

2½ cups water

¼ cup rosewater

1 cup sugar

½ tablespoon unsalted butter

1 cup unsweetened shredded coconut

½ cup walnut halves

Preparation

Mix together the wheat starch, water, and rosewater in a medium saucepan until the wheat starch has dissolved. Put the pan over medium heat and add the sugar and butter. Stir constantly and cook 17-22 minutes or until the mixture is thick and turns into a paste. Turn off the heat and set the paste aside. Spread the shredded coconut on a plate. Use a spoon to roll up a small ball of the paste, then drop it into the coconut, and roll until it's completely coated. Place the ball on a serving plate and press a walnut half on top. Repeat with the remaining paste, coconut, and walnut halves. Store the candies in the refrigerator.

Persian Rosettes

Preparation time: 5 minutes
Cook time: 30 minutes
Nutrition facts: Calories 170/ carbs 27 g/Fat 9 g /Protein 2 g

Ingredients (6 servings)

⅓ cup wheat starch

4 tablespoons rosewater

3 large eggs

⅓ cup all-purpose flour

½ cup vegetable oil for frying, plus more if needed

Powdered sugar

Preparation

Mix rosewater and wheat starch and in a large bowl until it forms a paste. Add the eggs and beat until they are fully combined. Add the flour and mix until the batter is smooth. Let the batter sit at room temperature for 35 minutes before frying. Heat the oil in a small saucepan until bubbles form around a toothpick touching the bottom of the pan. Heat the rosette iron by putting it in the hot oil for 10 seconds. Lift the iron, shake off the excess oil, and immediately dip it into the batter, just enough so that the edge of the iron is even with the surface of the batter. There shouldn't be any batter on the upper surface of the iron. Once the iron is coated with batter, dip it back into the hot oil, let the rosette puff and drop off the iron, and then take the iron out of the oil. Using tongs or chopsticks, fry the rosette on each side for 30 seconds or until golden brown. Immediately remove the rosette from the oil and place it on paper towels to drain. Repeat with the remaining batter. When all the rosettes are ready, let them cool a bit, then dust them with powdered sugar.

Roasted Chickpea Flour Cookies

Preparation time: 10 minutes
Cook time: 20 minutes
Nutrition facts: Calories 79/ carbs 6 g/Fat 6 g /Protein 1 g

Ingredients (10 servings)

9 ounces vegetable shortening

2 cups powdered sugar

1 pound roasted chickpea flour

1 teaspoon ground cardamom

2 tablespoons all-purpose flour

1 tablespoon ground pistachios

Preparation

Combine the shortening and powdered sugar in a large bowl and beat the mixture with an electric mixer or a wire whisk until it turns a light cream color. Add the cardamom, chickpea flour and all-purpose flour to the bowl and stir gently until all the ingredients are well incorporated. Divide the dough in half and shape each half into discs. Wrap the discs in plastic and refrigerate the dough for at least 13 hours.

Preheat the oven to 350 F. Line two baking sheets with parchment paper. Take the dough out of the refrigerator and let it sit for 20 minutes to come to room temperature. Dust just a little flour on a rolling pin and roll out one dough disc to a ½-inch thickness. Use a cookie cutter to cut it into shapes. Place the cookies on one of the prepared baking sheets. Repeat with the second disc. Sprinkle the ground pistachios over the cookies. Bake for 17 minutes or until the bottoms are very light brown. Remove the cookies from the oven and let them cool on the baking sheets for about 25 minutes and then serve.

Rice Flour Cookies

Preparation time: 20 minutes

Cook time: 15 minutes

Nutrition facts: Calories 39/ carbs 6 g/Fat 2 g /Protein 1 g

Ingredients (10 servings)

1¾ cups powdered sugar

1 pound rice flour

9 ounces vegetable shortening

2 large eggs

1 tablespoon rosewater

1 teaspoon ground cardamom

1 tablespoon poppy seeds

Preparation

Sift the powdered sugar and rice flour separately into different bowls. Combine the shortening and powdered sugar and beat them together using a mixer or a wire whisk until the mixture turns a light cream color. Add the eggs, one at a time, and beat them until fully combined and then mix in the rosewater. Add the rice flour to the mixture and mix gently until all the ingredients are well incorporated. Divide the dough in half and shape each half into a disc. Wrap the discs in plastic and refrigerate the dough for at least 13 hours.

Preheat the oven to 350 F. Line two baking sheets with parchment paper. Take the dough out of the refrigerator and leave it at the room temperature for 25 minutes. Pull off small pieces of dough and use your hands to shape them into balls. Place the cookies on the baking sheets, press them gently with a cookie stamp or the back of a spoon, and sprinkle them with the poppy seeds. Bake for 15 minutes, until the bottoms are very light brown. Remove the cookies from the oven and let them cool on the baking sheets for about 25 minutes and serve.

Persian Crepes With Syrup

Preparation time: 5 minutes

Cook time: 10 minutes

Nutrition facts: Calories 276/ carbs 37 g/Fat 13 g /Protein 4 g

Ingredients (4 servings)

2 large eggs

2 tablespoons whole milk

2 tablespoons all-purpose flour

1 tablespoon vegetable oil

½ cup grape molasses

Preparation

Crack the eggs into a large bowl and beat them with an electric mixer or wire whisk until foamy. Add the milk and flour and beat until everything is well combined and the batter is smooth. Heat the vegetable oil in a large nonstick skillet over medium heat. Pour all of the batter into the pan and cook for 3 minutes on each side or until golden brown. Using a spatula, cut the crêpe into eight wedges in the pan and pour the molasses over the top. Reduce the heat to low and cook for 1 minute, until the crêpe has absorbed the molasses.

Pumpkin Pancakes

Preparation time: 5 minutes

Cook time: 30 minutes

Nutrition facts: Calories 278/ carbs 46 g/Fat 7 g /Protein 8 g

Ingredients (6 servings)

½ cup sugar

1 large egg, at room temperature

3 tablespoons rosewater

1 cup pumpkin purée

1 cup all-purpose flour

1 teaspoon baking powder

½ teaspoon ground cinnamon

2 tablespoons vegetable oil

1 tablespoon powdered sugar

½ cup chopped walnuts and pistachios

Preparation

Combine the sugar and egg in a large bowl and beat them together using an electric mixer or wire whisk. Add the rosewater and pumpkin purée and beat until smooth. Add the flour, baking powder, and cinnamon, and mix well. Let the batter sit in the refrigerator 55-65 minutes. Heat the vegetable oil in a large nonstick skillet over medium heat. Pour in ¼ cup of batter for each pancake. Cook each pancake for 3 minutes per side, until they're browned and springy to the touch. Serve warm topped with powdered walnuts, sugar, and pistachios.

Saffron Syrup Cake

Preparation time: 65 minutes

Cook time: 20 minutes

Nutrition facts: Calories 325/ carbs 51 g/Fat 21 g /Protein 5 g

Ingredients (8 servings)

Cake

1 cup whole milk

1 tablespoon freshly squeezed lemon juice

4 large eggs, at room temperature

1 cup sugar

½ cup vegetable oil

2 cups all-purpose flour

1½ teaspoons baking powder

1 teaspoon ground cardamom

2 tablespoons ground pistachios

3 tablespoons unsweetened shredded coconut

Syrup

1 cup sugar

1 cup water

4 tablespoons bloomed saffron

2 tablespoons rosewater

Preparation

Cake

Preheat the oven to 350F. Line a 9 x 13-inch baking dish with parchment paper. Mix the milk and lemon juice in a small bowl. Set it aside for 7 minutes. In a large bowl, using a mixer or a wire whisk, beat the eggs until foamy. Add sugar and continue until it is fully combined and then add the oil and the lemon juice and milk mixture. Beat for 1 minute. Add the flour, baking powder, and ground cardamom. Stir gently using a spatula until just combined. Pour the batter in the baking dish that has been prepared and bake for 25 minutes or until a tester toothpick comes out clean.

Syrup
While the cake bakes, combine the sugar and water in a small saucepan over medium heat. Bring the mixture to a simmer, stirring frequently, then stir in the bloomed saffron and rosewater. Simmer for 2-3 minutes, then remove the pan from heat. Let the syrup cool to room temperature. Ensure both the cake and the syrup are at room temperature before cutting the cake.

Remove the cake from the oven and let it cool to room temperature. When the cake is cool, use a sharp knife to cut it into 1½-inch-wide strips, then cut on the diagonal so you have diamond-shaped cake pieces. Don't take the pieces out of the pan. Gently spoon the cooled syrup slowly over the cake. The cake will absorb the syrup right away. Use enough syrup so every part of the cake is soaked, but don't use so much that it's soggy. Top the cake with the ground pistachios and shredded coconut. Gently take the cake pieces out of the baking pan and place them on individual plates.

Bamieh

Preparation time: 40 minutes
Cook time: 10 minutes
Nutrition facts: Calories 296/ carbs 57 g/Fat 8 g /Protein 1 g

Ingredients (4 servings)
3 tablespoons of rosewater
5 tablespoons of cooking oil
½ pound of granulated sugar
3 eggs
¼ pound of all-purpose flour

Preparation
Mix 2 teaspoons sugar with 1 cup of water and cooking oil and bring to boil. Pour flour in and combine well. When water has boiled off, and mixture has thickened, remove from the burner. Allow mixture to cool and then add eggs. Combine well. Heat oil in pan until it is hot. Pour mixture through funnel into pan, thus creating flat balls each of about 1 ¼ inches diameter. Fry both sides of balls for 11-13 minutes. Mix cup of water with 2 teaspoons of sugar and rosewater. Heat until the water has boiled, and syrup has thickened. Remove from burner. Soak doughnuts (bamieh) in syrup for 7 minutes.

Brown Sugar Shortbread

Preparation time: 80 minutes

Cook time: 45 minutes

Nutrition facts: Calories 230/ carbs 22 g/Fat 16 g /Protein 2 g

Ingredients (16 servings)

1/3 cup of semi-sweet chocolate morsels

2 cups of all-purpose flour

¾ cup of packed brown sugar

1 cup of softened butter

Preparation

Preheat the oven to 325 F. Grease 9-inch round cake pan and set it aside. Beat sugar and butter with electric mixer in a large-sized bowl until the mixture is fluffy and light. Add flour gradually. Beat on low until well-blended. Spread in prepared pan and press into an even layer. Lightly cut surface with a knife into wedges. Bake for 40-50 minutes or until cake is golden. Cool for 20 minutes on a wire rack. Remove from the pan to finish cooling. Pour the melted chocolate morsels in small plastic bag. Snip across one corner to make a tiny spout. Drizzle it over the shortbread and then cut into wedges.

Pound Cake

Preparation time: 85 minutes

Cook time: 50 minutes

Nutrition facts: Calories 130/ carbs 20 g/Fat 7 g /Protein 2 g

Ingredients (6 servings)

3 large eggs

¼ teaspoons vanilla extract

1½ teaspoons rosewater

1/3 cup softened butter

½ one 8-oz. package softened cream cheese

1 cup granulated sugar

¼ teaspoons coarse salt

½ teaspoons ground cardamom

1 teaspoon baking powder

½ cup almond flour

1 cup all-purpose flour

Non-stick spray

Preparation

Preheat the oven to 325 F. Spray Bundt pan with non-stick spray. Line with bakery paper and spray the paper, as well. Whisk salt, cardamom, baking powder, almond flour and all-purpose flour together in medium bowl. Combine butter, sugar, and cream cheese in bowl. Beat with electric mixer until the mixture is fluffy and light. Add vanilla extract and rosewater. Add eggs slowly and beat well after each one. Beat this mixture on low speed gradually until the batter becomes smooth and with no lumps. Pour the batter into Bundt pan. Bake in oven for 60 minutes or until toothpick inserted into middle of cake come back clean. Cool for 15 minutes and then invert onto a wire rack to finish cooling. Slice and serve.

Persian Ice Cream (*Bastani Akbar-Mashti*)

Preparation time: 5 minutes

Nutrition facts: Calories 220/ carbs 27 g/Fat 11 g /Protein 3 g

Ingredients (4 servings)

2 tablespoons rosewater

¼ pound heavy double cream

32 ounces vanilla ice cream

Preparation

Leave double cream in your freezer until it has frozen completely. The ice cream and cream should not be too hard. Cut the frozen cream into cubes. Mix with the ice cream. Add the rosewater. Mix to combine and place in freezer for at least 70 minutes.

Persian Cupcakes (*Yazdi Cakes*)

Preparation time: 15 minutes
Cook time: 30 minutes
Nutrition facts: Calories 120/ carbs 56 g/Fat 16 g /Protein 4 g

Ingredients (24 servings)

1 cup white flour
1 cup rice flour
1 teaspoon baking powder
4 eggs
1 1/3 cups white sugar
1 cup melted butter
1 cup Greek Vanilla yogurt
1 tablespoon cardamom
2 tablespoon rose water
¾ cup chopped walnuts

Preparation

Preheat the oven to 350 F. Combine the white flour, rice flour, and baking soda in a bowl. Lightly grease a muffin pan with 24 cups or use 2 muffin pans. Whisk the eggs and sugar in a top of a double boiler with simmer water for 9-10 minutes. Remove the bowl from double boiler and keep mixing for 13-15 minutes. Stir in the butter, rose water, vanilla yogurt, and cardamom. Combine the yogurt mixture with the flour mixture. Stir in the chopped walnuts. Fill the muffin pan with the batter and bake for 30 minutes.

Persian Walnut Cookies

Preparation time: 10 minutes
Cook time: 15 minutes
Nutrition facts: Calories 30/ carbs 7 g/Fat 0 g /Protein 0 g

Ingredients (36 servings)

1 ¾ cups ground walnuts

3 egg yolks

2/3 cup sugar

1 tablespoon vanilla extract

1 egg white

½ cup halved walnuts

Preparation

Preheat the oven to 350 F. Combine the egg yolks, ground walnuts, sugar and vanilla extract in a bowl. Create small balls and transfer to a baking sheet covered with parchment. Whisk the egg white and brush over the cookies. Insert a walnut half in the center of each cookie. Bake for 17 minutes but start checking after 11 minutes. Cool and serve.

Persian Cookies

Preparation time: 10 minutes

Cook time: 20 minutes

Nutrition facts: Calories 79/ carbs 6 g/Fat 6 g /Protein 1 g

Ingredients (32 servings)

2 cups finely chopped almond

5 egg yolks

1 cup sugar

1 teaspoon cinnamon

1 teaspoon nutmeg

1 teaspoon baking soda

1 teaspoon almond extract

2 teaspoon lemon juice

1/3 cup chopped almonds

Preparation

Preheat the oven to 350 F. Combine sugar, almonds, 4 egg yolks, lemon juice, cinnamon, nutmeg, baking soda and almond extract using mixer. Line a baking sheet with parchment paper. Roll the teaspoon-sized balls in the chopped almonds and place them on the baking sheet with 2 inches between them. Combine 1 egg yolk with 1 teaspoon of water. Brush the cookie balls with the egg yolk glaze and bake for 22 minutes.

Persian Almond Cake

Preparation time: 15 minutes

Cook time: 20 minutes

Nutrition facts: Calories 241/ carbs 12 g/Fat 65g /Protein 5 g

Ingredients (25 servings)

½ teaspoon ground saffron

3 tablespoon rose water

1 teaspoon lemon zest

2 tablespoon butter

2 cups sugar

1 teaspoon vanilla extract

10 cups almond flour

¼ cup chopped pistachios

1 teaspoon cardamom

Salt to taste

Preparation

Line a 9x13 inch baking pan with parchment paper and butter the paper. Add 1 cup of water and the sugar to a pan and bring to a boil. Stir in the rose water, saffron, lemon zest, and vanilla extract. Remove from heat and let cool. Place the syrup in a stand mixer and best for 2-3 minutes. Gradually add the almond flour to create a paste and season with salt. Pour the paste in the baking pan and flatten for a 2-inch thickness. Refrigerate for 24 hours. Cut the cake into 25 diamond shaped pieces. Combine the pistachios and cardamom in a bowl and top each cake piece with the pistachio mixture.

Persian Walnut Cake

Preparation time: 10 minutes
Cook time: 20 minutes
Nutrition facts: Calories 160/ carbs 24 g/Fat 6g /Protein 3 g

Ingredients (4 servings)

3 cup, pitted dates
1 ½ cup, sifted all-purpose flour
½ cup, powdered sugar
1 teaspoon ground cinnamon
½ teaspoon ground cardamom
1 cup, pistachios, ground unsalted
1 cup, walnuts, coarsely chopped
1 cup unsalted butter
Dough

Preparation

In a large skillet toast the walnuts for 6-7 minutes and then place them aside. Place some walnuts in the middle of the dates and lay them in the bottom of a serving dish. Put a large pan over medium heat and cook the flour with butter for 18-20 minutes or until they become golden brown over high heat. Pour the hot mix all over the dates and spread it. In a small mixing bowl, mix in it the cinnamon, sugar and cardamom. Sprinkle the mix all over the butter and flour layer, followed by the pistachios. Place the cake aside to lose heat and add your preferred topping to taste.

Persian Rice Cookies

Preparation time: 15 minutes

Cook time: 10 minutes

Nutrition facts: Calories 120/ carbs 18 g/Fat 4 g /Protein 2 g

Ingredients (90 servings)

Syrup

¼ teaspoon rosewater

¾ cup sugar

Cookies

1 cup rice flour

1/3 clarified butter

1 egg yolk

¾ teaspoon sugar

1 tablespoon poppy seeds

½ cardamom powder

2 ½ canola oil

¼ cup syrup

Preparation

Syrup

Pour the sugar and ¼ cup water into a saucepan over high heat. Mix the content 4-6 minutes or until the sugar melts. Take the pan away from the heat, add rosewater, and allow it cool down.

Cookies

Preheat the oven to 350F. Put the egg yolk and sugar into a bowl and mix until they blend consistently and then leave aside. Add clarified butter to another bowl together with oil, rice flour and cardamom. Pour the sugar and yolk mixture into the bowl and make sure they're evenly mixed and blended. Include the syrup and mix again. Let it cool. Mold the mixture into balls and put on a parchment paper-lined baking sheet. The balls should be about 1/8 pounds and should be about ¾ inches thick. Flatten the balls by using a meat mallet or a fork. Scatter poppy seeds on them and bake for 11-13 minutes or until done. Cool down before serving.

Appetizers and Dips

Yogurt and Cucumber

Preparation time: 10 minutes

Nutrition facts: Calories 107/ carbs 13 g/Fat 3 g /Protein 9 g

Ingredients (4 servings)

2 Persian cucumbers or any seedless cucumbers

3 cups plain Greek yogurt

3 tablespoons chopped walnuts, divided

2 tablespoons raisins, divided

½ teaspoon salt

1 tablespoon dried mint, plus more for garnish

Preparation

Cut the cucumbers into quarters lengthwise, and then chop them into very small pieces. In a large bowl, mix together the chopped cucumber, yogurt, 2 tablespoons of chopped walnuts, 1 tablespoon of raisins, the salt, and the dried mint. Garnish with the remaining 1 tablespoon of walnuts and 1 tablespoon of raisins and some more dried mint. Serve immediately.

Yogurt and Eggplant

Preparation time: 15 minutes
Cook time: 30 minutes
Nutrition facts: Calories 44/ carbs 6 g/Fat 5 g /Protein 4 g

Ingredients (4 servings)

2 large eggplants
2 garlic cloves, minced
3 cups plain Greek yogurt
1 tablespoon olive oil
1 onion, thinly sliced
½ teaspoon salt
½ teaspoon freshly ground black pepper

Preparation

Preheat the oven to 425 F. Line a baking sheet with aluminum foil and coat it with nonstick cooking spray. Pierce the eggplants a few times with a fork. Place them on the prepared baking sheet and roast them in the oven for 32-35 minutes or until they're fully cooked, and the skin is wrinkled. Remove the eggplants from the oven and let them cool completely. As the eggplants are roasting, heat the olive oil over medium heat in a medium skillet and cook the onion and garlic for 11-13 minutes or until tender and golden brown. Peel the eggplants and chop them very finely.

In a large bowl, mix together the chopped eggplant, caramelized onion and garlic, yogurt, salt, and pepper. Cover the bowl and let the mixture chill in the refrigerator for 30-35 minutes before serving.

Yogurt and Zucchini

Preparation time: 10 minutes

Nutrition facts: Calories 100/ carbs 19 g/Fat 1.5 g /Protein 2 g

Ingredients (4 servings)

2 zucchinis

2 cups plain Greek yogurt

¼ teaspoon salt

¼ teaspoon freshly ground black pepper

½ teaspoon garlic powder

1 tablespoon chopped fresh mint

Preparation

Grate the zucchini. Squeeze it well in a clean kitchen towel or place it in a fine-mesh colander and press on it with the back of a wooden spoon. Discard the excess water. In a separate bowl, mix together the yogurt, grated zucchini, salt, pepper, garlic powder, and mint. Cover the bowl and let the mixture chill in the refrigerator for 30 to 40 minutes before serving.

Lime Pickle (*Torshi limoo*)

Preparation time: 20 minutes

Nutrition facts: Calories 191/ carbs 3 g/Fat 17 g /Protein 0 g

Ingredients (2 servings)

1 tablespoon salt

1 tablespoon red pepper

10 limes

Lemon juice

Preparation

Wash the limes and cut in halves and put in a small container. Add pepper and salt. Pour in the lemon juice to fill up the container and cover with its lid. Keep the jar in a cool room temperature and leave for 30 days, before serving.

Potatoes Patties (*Kookoo Sip Zamini*)

Preparation time: 10 minutes

Cook time: 10 minutes

Nutrition facts: Calories 130/ carbs 17 g/Fat 7 g /Protein 1 g

Ingredients (4 servings)

3 eggs

5 boiled and smashed potatoes

½ teaspoon turmeric

¼ teaspoon black pepper

½ teaspoon salt

Oil

Preparation

Combine the potatoes, eggs, turmeric, salt, and pepper in a bowl and mix thoroughly. Pour 5 teaspoon oil into a large pan and heat over medium heat. Mold potato mixture into round shapes and flatten them. Put them into the pan with caution and fry for 13 minutes. When the bottom turns golden brown, flip the patties over. Grab a dish and a paper towel. Make sure you remove as much oil as you can from the patties. Transfer to the plate and serve.

Cucumber Yogurt (*Maast-o Khiar*)

Preparation time: 70 minutes

Nutrition facts: Calories 55/ carbs 6 g/Fat 3 g /Protein 3 g

Ingredients (14 servings)

2 cup plain Greek yogurt

3 peeled and diced cucumbers

2 tablespoons diced onions

3 tablespoons dill

1 teaspoon mint

3 tablespoons chopped walnuts

Salt and pepper to taste

Preparation

Combine the ingredients and refrigerate for at least 70 minutes and serve.

Persian Bread (*Lavosh*)

Preparation time: 5 minutes
Cook time: 10 minutes
Nutrition facts: Calories 110/ carbs 22 g/Fat 1g /Protein 4 g

Ingredients (10 servings)

2½ cups flour

3 tablespoons melted butter

2 tablespoons grated parmesan cheese

2 teaspoons sugar

Dash of salt

3 egg whites

Preparation

Preheat the oven to 400 F. Mix flour, salt and sugar in a bowl. Stir in ¾ cup of water, egg white and the melted butter and combine until dough is created. Knead the dough for 7 minutes and Create 10 separate ball and roll each ball as thin as possible and transfer to a baking sheet. Brush the lavosh with beaten egg white, salt, and parmesan cheese. Bake for 12 minutes and serve.

Spinach Pancake

Preparation time: 10 minutes

Cook time: 20 minutes

Nutrition facts: Calories 294/ carbs 19 g/Fat 10g /Protein 5 g

Ingredients (2 servings)

4 eggs

¼ cup unsalted butter, divided

¼ parsley, chopped

4 scallions, chopped

½ oz spinach, stems removed and chopped

Salt

Black pepper

Preparation

In a skillet, melt 3 tablespoons of butter over medium heat. Add the parsley and cook for 3-4 minutes. Ensure that you stir at intervals until the scallions become softer. Add the spinach and place a cover on the skillet. Continue to cook for 6 minutes or until it begins to wilt. Remove the cover and continue to cook. Mix the content intermittently over the next 22-26 minutes or until the flavors blend. Meanwhile, break the egg into a bowl and whisk with an electric mixer until the texture becomes thick, and the color light.

Pour the spinach mixture into the eggs and mix. Add salt and black pepper to your taste. In a 10-inch skillet and melt the remaining butter portion over medium heat. Pour the egg mixture into it. Place a cover on it and cook for 11-14 minutes. Use a spatula to loosen the edge of the pancakes and transfer into a plate.

Persian sesame bread

Preparation time: 10 minutes

Cook time: 20 minutes

Nutrition facts: Calories 140/ carbs 28 g/Fat 2g /Protein 6 g

Ingredients (3 servings)

1 pound flour

2 oz fresh yeast

1 ½ cup warm water

1 tablespoon brown sugar

1 teaspoon salt

4 tablespoon olive oil

2 tablespoon corn flour (optional)

1 teaspoon black sesame

Preparation

In a large mixing bowl mix in it the flour with corn flour and a pinch of salt. Make a small well in the middle of the flour mix. Place in it the sugar with yeast and 5 tablespoon of warm water and mix them well. Place it on the side with a kitchen towel to cover it for 32-35 minutes. Add the rest of the water and water then mix them again until you get a smooth dough. Place it aside to rest for 70 minutes and preheat the oven to 400 F. Shape the dough into several circles of flat bread and place them on lined up baking sheet. Brush them with olive oil and top them with sesame seeds. Cook them in the oven for 15 to 18 min and serve.

Persian Potato Frittata

Preparation time: 5 minutes
Cook time: 10 minutes
Nutrition facts: Calories 205/ carbs 6 g/Fat 15g /Protein 11 g

Ingredients (3 servings)

7 potatoes, peeled and shredded
¼ cup vegetable oil
1 shredded onion
2 eggs
1 tablespoon of margarine
½ teaspoon of mint
Salt and pepper to taste
Turmeric

Preparation

Preheat the oven to 400 F. Grease a casserole dish with some butter. In a large mixing bowl mix the potatoes, onion, eggs, salt, pepper, turmeric, and mint. Pour the vegetable oil over medium heat and heat until it starts sizzling. Pour the potato mix into the casserole dish. Drizzle the hot oil all over it. Place it in the oven and cook it for 11-13 minutes.

Persian Trail Mix (*Ajil*)

Preparation time: 10 minutes
Cook time: 18 minutes
Nutrition facts: Calories 360/ carbs 57 g/Fat 25 g /Protein 4 g

Ingredients (5 servings)

1 cup whole salted pistachios
1 cup pumpkin seeds, roasted and salted
½ cup almonds, roasted and unsalted
2/3 cup mulberries, dried
½ cup chickpeas, dried and salted
½ cup currants, dried
½ cup golden raisins
8 Mission figs, dried
8 Turkish figs, dried

Preparation

Mix all ingredients in a bowl and combine together thoroughly. Keep in an airtight container for about two weeks.

Falafel

Preparation time: 10 minutes
Cook time: 30 minutes
Nutrition facts: Calories 176/ carbs 10 g/Fat 13 g /Protein 4 g

Ingredients (5 servings)

2 cups chickpeas, soaked

3 cloves garlic

1 onion, chopped

1 tablespoon baking powder

2 tablespoon sesame seeds

1 teaspoon salt

½ teaspoon pepper

Oil

Water

Preparation

Soak the chickpeas, preferably through the night, to increase the yield. Remove the water and wash with fresh water and then put in a food processor. Add the onion and garlic cloves and grind the content until the mixture becomes a paste, but not pureed. Add water if too dry. Add baking powder, salt, pepper, and sesame seeds and mix together. Wrap the opening of the bowl with a foil and put into the fridge for 100 minutes. Line a non-stick skillet with vegetable oil to about an inch and put it over medium heat. As you do this, mold the mixture into round balls. With caution, put them into the oil and fry until they turn golden-brown. Flip to the other sides and fry until the same thing happens. After both sides have turned golden-brown, take them away and serve.

Sweet Persian Pastry (*Nazook*)

Preparation time: 10 minutes
Cook time: 25 minutes
Nutrition facts: Calories 290/ carbs 40 g/Fat 13 g /Protein 4 g

Ingredients (10 servings)

Dough

2 teaspoons white sugar

1 cup sour cream

1 cup package active dry yeast

1 egg

1 tablespoon oil

3 cups flour

1 tablespoon white vinegar

½ cup butter

Filling

2 ½ cups white sugar

1 pound butter (melted)

4 cups flour

2 egg whites

2 teaspoons vanilla extract

Glaze

1 teaspoon plain yogurt

2 egg yolks

Preparation

Pour the sour cream, yeast, and sugar into a bowl and mix. Leave for 5 minutes and then add vinegar, oil, and egg. Put 3 cups of flour in another bowl. Add ½ cup butter, integrating it with the flour until the mixture is evenly blended. Go back to the sour cream combination and stir until occasionally until the dough blends together. Bring the dough out and place it on a floured workstation. Knead and press until it's smooth but still sticky; this could take up to 12 minutes. Use a knife to cut out the dough into four pieces and cover each of them with a plastic wrap or foil. Put them inside the refrigerator for at least 130 minutes.

Filling

Preheat oven to 350F. Mix the melted butter, vanilla extract, and sugar in a bowl. Put in 4 cups flour and stir. Add the egg whites and mix, too. Take a piece of the dough and roll it into a rectangle (8 x 12 inch). Disperse a quarter of the filling combination on top of it. Use a plastic wrap to cover the filling and with a rolling pin, flatten it out. Turn the dough into a firm roll, beginning from one of the long sides. Slice the roll into a 2-inch bit. Put the bits on a rimmed baking sheet. Gently press from the top to flatten. Do this for the other 3 pieces of dough and filling.

Glaze

Beat the yogurt and egg yolk together to make the glaze. Line the glaze on pieces of the dough. Put in the preheated oven and bake for 26-32 minutes or until they turn golden brown. Leave to cool before serving.

Eggplant Dip (Kashk-e Bademjan)

Preparation time: 10 minutes

Cook time: 25 minutes

Nutrition facts: Calories 263/ carbs 21 g/Fat 20 g /Protein 4 g

Ingredients (4 servings)

1 onion

6 eggplants

5 cloves garlic

1 teaspoon salt

1 teaspoon turmeric

1 tablespoon mint (chopped)

1 cup *kashk*

½ cups walnut

Oil

Preparation

Remove the top and skin of the eggplants and cut into half. Pour oil into a frying pan and fry the eggplants until it changes to golden and is soft; then remove from the frying pan. Cut the garlic and onions and put them inside a frying pan with heated oil. Add turmeric, mint, and salt before mixing together. Go back to the fried eggplant and add them to the mixture. Pour ½ cup of water and leave to cook for 17 minutes over medium heat. Break the walnuts and add to the mixture. Pound it until the mixture becomes smooth. Pour into a bowl and pour *kashk*. Top with walnuts and fried onions.

If you liked Persian food, discover to how cook *DELICIOUS* recipes from other Balkan countries!

Within these pages, you'll learn 35 authentic recipes from a Balkan cook. These aren't ordinary recipes you'd find on the Internet, but recipes that were closely guarded by our Balkan mothers and passed down from generation to generation.

Main Dishes, Appetizers, and Desserts included!

If you want to learn how to make Croatian green peas stew, and 32 other authentic Balkan recipes, then start with our book!

Available at Amazon for only $2,99!

If you're a Mediterranean dieter who wants to know the secrets of the Mediterranean diet, dieting, and cooking, then you're about to discover how to master cooking meals on a Mediterranean diet right now!

In fact, if you want to know how to make Mediterranean food, then this new e-book - "The 30-minute Mediterranean diet" - gives you the answers to many important questions and challenges every Mediterranean dieter faces, including:

How can I succeed with a Mediterranean diet?

What kind of recipes can I make?

What are the key principles to this type of diet?

What are the suggested weekly menus for this diet?

Are there any cheat items I can make?

... and more!

If you're serious about cooking meals on a Mediterranean diet and you really want to know how to make Mediterranean food, then you need to grab a copy of "The 30-minute Mediterranean diet" right now.

Prepare **111 recipes with several ingredients in less than 30 minutes**!

Available at Amazon for only $2,99!

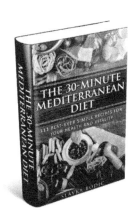

What could be better than a home-cooked meal? Maybe only a Greek homemade meal.

Do not get discouraged if you have no Greek roots or friends.

Now you can make a Greek food feast in your kitchen.

This ultimate Greek cookbook offers you 111 best dishes of this cuisine! From more famous gyros to more exotic *Kota Kapama* this cookbook keeps it easy and affordable.

All the ingredients necessary are wholesome and widely accessible.

The author's picks are as flavorful as they are healthy. The dishes described in this cookbook are "what Greek mothers have made for decades."

Full of well-balanced and nutritious meals, this handy cookbook includes many vegan options.
Discover a plethora of benefits of Mediterranean cuisine, and you may fall in love with cooking at home.

Inspired by a real food lover, this collection of delicious recipes will taste buds utterly satisfied.

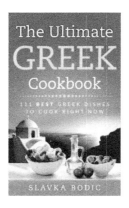

Available at Amazon for only $2,99!

Maybe to try exotic Serbian cuisine?

From succulent sarma, soups, warm and cold salads to delectable desserts, the plethora of flavors will satisfy the most jaded foodie. Have a taste of a new culture with this **traditional Serbian cookbook.**

Available at Amazon for only $2,99!

ONE LAST THING

If you enjoyed this book or found it useful I'd be very grateful if you could find the time to post a short review on Amazon. Your support really does make a difference and I read all the reviews personally, so I can get your feedback and make this book even better.

Thanks again for your support!

Please send me your feedback at

www.balkanfood.org

Made in the USA
Las Vegas, NV
08 April 2024

88422581R00098